Fraser Dyer is an Anglican  in the author of *Why Do I Do Th*. *Work* (Lion, 2005).

# WHO ARE WE TO JUDGE?

*Empathy and discernment in a critical age*

Fraser Dyer

First published in Great Britain in 2015

Society for Promoting Christian Knowledge
36 Causton Street
London SW1P 4ST
www.spck.org.uk

British Library Cataloguing-in-Publication Data
A catalogue record for this book is available from the British Library

ISBN 978–0–281–07248–4
eBook ISBN 978–0–281–07249–1

Typeset by Graphicraft Limited, Hong Kong
First printed in Great Britain by Ashford Colour Press
Subsequently digitally printed in Great Britain

eBook by Graphicraft Limited, Hong Kong

Produced on paper from sustainable forests

# Contents

—•◆•—

# Contents

## Part 3
## TOWARDS DISCERNMENT

# Acknowledgements

I am grateful to James Ashdown, Lucyann Ashdown, Sean Cathie, Geoffrey Court, Lincoln Harvey and Alison Lyon, who were generous with their time and their advice; and to the Sisters of Perpetual Encouragement: Helen Hancock, Wendy Harvey, Jane Hodges, Alison Kennedy, Penny Rose-Casemore and Tim Jeffries. Sinclair Dyer and Jane Wenlock both gave me books and, in so doing, introduced me to the works of Francis Spufford and Cynthia Bourgeault respectively. My former business partner Ursula Jost did much to help me think myself into the shoes of others, while Bob O'Dell introduced me to civil discourse. John Bailey, as ever, was in charge of stress management and sweeping up the breakages.

# Introduction

We begin with a mea culpa.

The first person to write a job reference for me memorably wrote, 'Fraser is not someone who suffers fools gladly.' I was 18 years old. I like to think I've mellowed in the intervening years, but this is delusional. I've simply become better at pretending I'm not bothered – and sometimes these days I just can't find the energy to get steamed up about things the way I used to.

The black and white certainties of youth have given way to a blizzard of grey. It's hard to get uppity about things when convictions have been battered by experience. Not that this stops me trying, but at least these days I heave myself on to my high horse much less frequently than in the past. I suppose that is the product of some kind of maturity.

I do notice in some older people a kind of generous grace that won't be riled, an acceptance that a lot of battles just aren't worth the puff and a discovery of the freedom that lies in simply letting other people's silliness wash over them.

I'm not there yet – and *if* my people skills have improved, my capacity to tolerate other people's silliness has not. It's perhaps surprising, then, that a few years ago I took Holy Orders in the Church of England. If there's one institution that's a magnet for 'other people's daftness', it's the Church – capital 'C'. (I don't for a minute single out the dear old C of E from other denominations, some of whom I've journeyed with along the way.)

Naturally, I've contributed more than my fair share of idiocy to proceedings. A sermon in which the congregation – well, certainly my mother – understood me to be saying that if you don't buy fairly traded products you'll go to hell; an early pioneering attempt at what we now call 'café-style' worship that was so heavy on the croissants and Sunday papers that we kind of forgot about the worship; or publicly declaring, rather too often, my view that the best solution to difficult parishioners would be a sniper in the bell tower.

Still, in spite of all that and a great deal else, nothing will more induce me to roll my eyes and mentally pack up shop than having to put up with other people's foolishness. And, naturally, my own brilliance is crippled by the impediment of others who are variously fatheads, stick-in-the-muds, retrogrades, weasels, killjoys, useless, feckless, a bit up themselves – and a list of other terms more common to my lexicon that can't be printed here. All of which I set down to impress upon you just how immensely qualified I am to write on the subject of judgementalism. I am a grand master.

As a card-carrying hypocrite to boot, I tend not to dwell too much on *my* judgemental streak, preferring instead to get annoyed by others' (psychologists have a name for this – more of which later). There is no better comfort to my own insufferable judgementalism than to find someone even worse than me upon whom to redirect my loathing of this trait. I've found the appalling judgementalism and hypocrisy of a certain mid-market tabloid newspaper particularly helpful in this regard: 'How can they be so two-faced?' Subtext: not like me (polishes imaginary halo).

Fortunately, I was stupid enough to tell several people I was planning to write this book. Once they'd quickly masked a look of wide-eyed astonishment they suggested I might have to 'own' my own judgementalism. So here we are – I'm all fessed up.

Not that this will stop me. Lately I've been put back in my box on a regular basis by a certain party in my household who responds to my latest damning tirade by quietly asking, 'So how's that book on judgementalism coming along?' 'Oh, right . . .'

So this book is something of a personal exploration of the subject. Rather in the style of Stella Gibbons' *Cold Comfort Farm*, I was tempted to asterisk those passages of the book that themselves lapse into judgementalism. But I'll leave you to flag those for yourself. Tempting as it may have been to fill the book with potshots at others, not least the Church, I've tried very hard to put my grown-up hat on and make sense of the issue. Why do we tend so easily towards judging others? How do we respond to teaching on the subject in Scripture – and especially the Gospels? And what can I do through my own spiritual life to keep the lid on my judgementalism?

I pray that you will read this book with yourself in mind and not be tempted into thoughts of, 'Oh yes, that is *so* like such-and-such.' And if you are, pray for that person, for yourself, and for me. God knows, we need it.

I've organized the book in three parts. The first part explores why we feel the urge to judge others. The second part examines Jesus' teaching on judgementalism and how his interactions with others were very different from the way the Church often behaves today. In the third part I consider how we might find a different way of being church, one notable for the absence of relentlessly trying to set others straight, while at the same time retaining a vital voice in challenging the injustices of the world around us.

# Part 1

# UNDERSTANDING JUDGEMENTALISM

---

'Why do you pass judgement on your brother or sister?'
*Romans 14.10*

# 1

## *The urge to judge*

————◦•◦————

An ageing pop star has his house searched by police investigating historical allegations of sexual misconduct with an underage boy. Although the singer is given no warning of the search taking place, the media are tipped off by police and his name is all over the internet within minutes. Before any formal charges are laid, and in spite of the celebrity's denial of any wrongdoing, users of Twitter share their judgements online. 'Can't say I'm surprised', says one. 'I knew he'd be the next celebrity to turn out to be a rapist or paedo', says another. 'Why do all these celebrities have to live like beasts?', says a third, before adding the menacing hashtag #MurderThem.

Reading about this story on social media is a depressing experience. While some commentators remind us that a person is innocent until proved guilty, the torrent of abuse, off-colour jokes and assumptions of guilt permeate the debate like a bad odour. An MP, remarking on the injustice of being judged guilty before any charge has been prosecuted, says, 'People have zero per cent of the facts and a hundred per cent of the opinions. It's quite wrong for people to prejudge.'[1]

But we do – all the time, in fact. Our brains are busy working away, constantly making assessments of other people and trying to determine whether we can trust them – or not. Do we like them, believe them or feel we can cooperate with them? And when people behave in a way that's out of kilter with who we are, we find ourselves trying to figure them out. When they transgress our values, customs, etiquette or social norms we wonder, 'What *is* it with them?'

There are good sociological reasons why our brains work this way. They're finely tuned to assess danger in a situation, including the people we encounter. You only need to walk down an unlit deserted street and notice a hooded figure appear in the opposite direction to feel your senses go into hyperdrive and understand that instinct has taken over.

Desmond and Mpho Tutu write:

> In the past our survival depended on recognizing and being suspicious of difference. If people were in and of our group, we could assume good intent. If people were not in and of our group, we would be safest to assume evil intentions.[2]

This is all very useful in a primitive monoculture, and if our capacity to judge other people stopped there, we'd be doing fine. But when we look further we begin to see what problems our tendency for judgement can create. We make decisions about other people without having all the facts; just a look or a remark can turn us off a person quite unjustifiably; an encounter with someone bearing a physical resemblance to someone in our past can create ill feeling. Because judgements we make frequently rest on too little information, we fill in the gaps ourselves, based on – well, on what?

Our drive to judge others moves beyond a reasonable need for safety to one of *competition* – that human compulsion to clamber to the top of the pile, often at the expense of others. Or as Eugene Peterson puts it, in his translation of Galatians 5.21, 'The vicious habit of depersonalizing everyone into a rival.'[3] Before long our judgementalism is about putting others down in order to elevate ourselves in front of friends or colleagues. This is not self-preservation but chipping away at the reputation of others we judge to be threats or obstacles.

What began as a useful mechanism for personal safety can become a corrosive and destructive social weapon. Some of us are worse in this than others of course, but who hasn't made a snap judgement about another person without hearing that little inner voice saying, 'You're being unfair' or 'You're being unkind'?

Our judgemental streak, then, is a spiritual matter. In our quest to be the best we can be, to journey towards wholeness, the way we behave towards others is paramount. For Christians this is particularly so, as we follow the teachings and example of one who has much to say against judging others. Yet looking at the Church today I can't say I observe that its most striking feature is an absence of judgementalism.

A member of my congregation wants to start a new project in the parish. I suggest she write a proposal for the PCC to discuss. 'What?' she exclaims. 'That useless lot. If you left it to them we'd never get anything done.'

A new person starts attending our services. He's come from another church, where he became unpopular for asking awkward questions – 'You need to leave', they'd told him; 'You have a spirit of disobedience.' (In fact he had a mental illness and needed support to get the right treatment.)

A homeless person starts sleeping in the churchyard. 'We can't let this go on. Look at the mess he's creating. How could he have allowed himself to get into this state? It's so irresponsible.'

These remarks were made *to* rather than by me. But they could easily have been my words – I've certainly said things very like that and seen the consequences of such ill-informed judgements.

When I make remarks like these I never give the object of my judgement the benefit of the doubt. Lobbing an opinion into a situation, like a hand grenade, seldom leads to greater understanding or enlightenment. I shut down possibilities and fail to spot potential or new opportunities because I haven't opened myself up to discerning what's really going on. There's no inquiry, no curiosity, no open-mindedness, no possibility for growth. It's simply destructive – the conversational equivalent of turning my back on someone and walking away.

It is also hugely self-regarding when we speak of others in such ways. We pretend to ourselves, and those we talk to, that we're in a fine position to judge; that we have the experience, knowledge, upbringing or skills to assess others and their situation; that we have *all* the facts at our disposal to deliver our verdict.

It's also damaging to others in the way it diminishes them, setting aside any notion that they're made in the image of God or that we're called to see the face of Christ in them. The hand of friendship, far from being stretched out, is thrust deep in our pockets. Problems aren't resolved properly, the marginalized become even more disengaged and the misunderstood more so.

Christians are themselves on the receiving end of much judgementalism, not least in the 'God debate' that has recently emerged from the writing of the so-called new atheists. We're told that our beliefs are worthy of ridicule; that we're hypocrites who have failed to live up to our principles; that our Scriptures are works of fiction. There's been no shortage of responses, the most entertaining of which return fire in the same polemic style.

One of the charges levelled at the judgement of fundamentalist atheists is that they've failed to educate themselves on rudimentary theology and that their own aggressive rhetoric is open to the same accusations they make of religious fundamentalists. Like many debates rooted in deeply held views, the God debate has been all heat and no light, and the judgementalism that's bandied back and forth – no matter how entertaining – does little to illuminate our understanding or build common ground. But then that's rather the point of 'debates' like this: it isn't about finding a way forward but simply about building support for our point of view while undermining our opponent's.

Some of this behaviour is present in everyday conversation. One of the ways we judge other people is by how we listen to them. Rather than listening with a view to understanding, we commit half our mind to hearing what's being said while the other half busies itself deciding if we agree or not. Often we've made up our mind before they've finished speaking. Sometimes we prejudge what we think they're about to say, not what they're actually trying to say. 'To retort without first listening is both foolish and embarrassing' (Proverbs 18.13, NJB).

Both the Bible and Christian teaching down the centuries have plenty to say about the folly of judgementalism. Indeed it is often portrayed as a burden. 'If you remove the yoke from among you, the pointing of the finger, the speaking of evil . . . then you shall take delight in the LORD' (Isaiah 58.9, 14).

Or consider this saying from the Desert Fathers: 'Abba John the Little said: We have abandoned a light burden, namely self-criticism, and taken up a heavy burden, namely self-justification.'[4]

We shall see later how self-justification is a key driver of judge-mental behaviour.

Francis de Sales, writing over 400 years ago, said:

'Judge not and you will not be judged,' says the Saviour of our souls; 'Condemn not and you will not be condemned.' Or as the apostle Paul wrote, 'Judge not, but wait for the Lord. He will bring to the light things now hidden in darkness, and disclose the secret purposes of the heart.' Rash judgements are most displeasing to God. People's judgements are rash because we are not meant to be one another's judges, and in so acting we usurp the prerogative of God. Their judgements are rash because so often they proceed from malice, from the impenetrable depths of the human heart. Indeed they are impertinent, because each of us should find sufficient employ-ment in sorting ourselves out without having time to judge our neighbours.[5]

That last point is easier said than done. Judgementalism is an indicator of the state of our relationship with God, a kind of public and visible thermometer that exposes how much we trust God. It is perhaps in this way that our judgement of others leads to our own judgement, because it reveals the state of our heart and the quality of our relationship with God. 'When we genuinely believe that inner transformation is God's work and not ours, we can put to rest our passion to set others straight', writes Richard Foster.[6]

Much of this I know and understand. And yet my trigger-happy tendency to judge others is not abated. I find this embarrassing because I now realize that my judgementalism says more about me and the state of my spiritual health than it does about those I criticize. Clearly there are some deeply embedded psychological habits and patterns that are hard to shake off – it is to these we now turn.

# 2

## *Tribalism*

———•◆•———

Humans are tribal people. We stick to those of our own kind, reserving some of our worst judgements and prejudices for those who are different, perhaps even stereotyping them to help box them into a particular set of predetermined judgements. (Indeed prejudice is a form of judgementalism where we simply lift opinions off the peg, without stopping to think or offer people the benefit of the doubt.) Our own sense of identity comes from the tribe(s) we belong to, which not only defines us by who we *are* but also who we are *not*. We might go so far as to say that much conflict is not so much a rejection of the other as an assertion of the self.

Where once humans went to war over territory or resources, many of the conflicts we see in the world today are fought over beliefs – religion, race, culture or values. Tribalism is still writ large across the pages of our newspapers as journalists report on these hostilities. What is it that we find so intolerable about people who are different?

According to the primatologist Frans de Waal,

> We belong to the category of animals known among zoologists as 'obligatory gregarious,' meaning that we have no option but to stick together. This is why fear of ostracism lurks in the corner of every human mind: being expelled is the worst thing than can befall us. It was so in biblical times, and it remains so today. Evolution has instilled a need to belong and to feel accepted. We are social to our core.[1]

If we are to find meaningful acceptance within a social group, it follows that others must be defined as outside that group. Somehow, belonging to the whole family of the human race is not enough for most of us. So my judgements and rejection of some people feed my sense of affiliation to my own group. I am not English, I'm Scottish; I am not black, I'm white; I am not Roman Catholic, I'm Anglican; I am not right-wing, I'm left-wing; I am not straight, I'm gay; I am not a baby boomer, I'm Generation X.

It isn't enough to label ourselves. Each tag brings with it a whole bag of assumptions, prejudices and judgements about those outside our group. These really help to cement our own sense of who we are. I won't list the things people might think about some of the above categories – just observe any prejudices your own mind suggests to you.

Any temptation to think that Western society today is somehow more sophisticated or multicultural than so-called primitive societies fails to recognize that, psychologically at least, we remain as tribal as ever. We have not shaken off the need to *belong* or the instinct to expel those who don't. Margaret Thatcher's famous question is never far from our minds: 'Is he one of us?'

What has perhaps become more sophisticated these days is the way such tribalism plays out in our lives. While many of us have learnt to shake off inherited values of sexism, racism, homophobia and so on, and have embraced more inclusive communities and churches, the tribal mindset still makes itself known in our judgementalism.

'Because of the deep insecurity of our society,' says Timothy Radcliffe, 'we seek the assurance of the like-minded. But no community of the like-minded is a sign of the kingdom of God.'[2]

Jesus' ministry focused on the Jews. His mission was to fulfil the promises God had made to Israel. Even so, the multitribal nature of the kingdom of God couldn't help itself from breaking out and revealing itself in his encounters with ethnic and religious outsiders. Think of the Roman centurion, the woman at the well or the Syrophoenician woman.

It would fall to the Apostles to do the follow-up work of bringing the good news to people outside the Jewish faith and working out the thorny issues of how they did Church together. Imagine all those clashing cultures and customs and beliefs, finding unity in the body of Christ. For all that the universal Church still struggles to get this right, we see in the Christian testament some great visions of the rainbow community of the kingdom of God. Consider Pentecost and the multiplicity of languages that are spoken when the Holy Spirit is received. Or the images in Revelation of a multitude 'from every nation, from all tribes and peoples and languages' worshipping together (Revelation 7.9).

While the kingdom of God charts a course to break down our tribalism, our humanity remains powerfully tuned to primal instincts that shun difference. Yet we humans also have the amazing capacity to change the way we think, to reprogramme ourselves to choose different responses. As we journey on the path towards wholeness, our Christian heritage and faith offer many tools and resources to help shape our behaviour, the better to reflect the image of the divine we all carry within us. The starting point is to 'know thyself'.

When it comes to judgementalism we must take note of what is going on in our minds the moment a judgement is formed. Richard Rohr explains:

> Ill will is a poison which, if you don't catch it in the first ten seconds, takes over. As soon as you make a harsh judgement, you have a critical attitude towards a person or group. Watch your mind. In the next ten seconds you'll create a storyline to justify that negative thought and then you're totally invested in it. You don't just think she's an ugly woman or he's a bad man, but you start thinking about what part of town he's from, what race she is a part of or what religion he's involved with, and you are justified in your ill will.[3]

What these kinds of judgements do is create a sense of separateness, where we build a world with ourselves at the centre, and anyone who is not of our world or is outside of it is judged inferior.

> For some reason, as soon as you compare and compete, as soon as you judge two things (don't believe me – watch your own mind), you judge one to be higher and one to be lower.

That moves you into delusion, [one of the] great poisons that destroy everything. It is a dualistic process that constantly knows things by comparison and competition.[4]

Rohr's point about dualism tells me something important about the way my mind works. The constant assessments our minds are making – often on autopilot – are *comparative*. Is this person my inferior or superior? How does this fit with that? Does your opinion fit with my worldview? Could I take him if this gets ugly? Can I out-argue her or should I back down now because she seems better informed? We're measuring people up – what they say and how they behave – all the time. It's quite exhausting.

But what yardstick am I using to make my comparisons? There are doubtless many, but the starting point is – me. Because, naturally, I believe *I am normal*. The values of my upbringing (deeply ingrained), my life experience, my ideals, cultural norms, personal preferences, aspirations and all the other psychological baggage I'm lugging around in my head all shape my outlook and my judgements. It is this distinct sense of self that I use to separate myself off from others. Judging folk is how we know who we are – or tell ourselves who we are. I am not you.

Sometimes we are very glad of that and at other times envious. We curry the attention of the people we aspire to be like or have as our friends, while looking down on those who remind us of the worst aspects of ourselves – or who simply seem just too different, a bit odd perhaps. Judge, judge, judge.

And if I judge people to be out of line and feel the compulsion to set them straight, what I'm really trying to do is make them be like me. If I care about them I seek to draw them back into my tribe, my definition of normality.

I used to run courses for people who themselves were learning to design and deliver professional development training. One of the issues we talked about is the difference between teaching children and adults. Children at a certain primary-school age become sponges for information. Any parent will recognize the phase when the 'Why?' questions start or when certain subjects becomes the focus of endless fascination – dinosaurs, outer space or ponies – and their kids just devour whatever information they can get their heads around. They have such curiosity and openness to new information.

Adults, by contrast, test what they listen to. How does what you are telling me fit with what I already know or believe? Does my experience bear out the truth of what you say? Can I imagine a way of making that work? It is because we do this as adults that much professional development training has moved away from traditional teaching and lecturing. When you give a straight presentation you have to overcome the obstacle of your audience's judgementalism. As they listen they are comparing what you say with what they know, or think they know. Have you ever noticed during a Q&A afterwards that mostly what is offered from the floor are not actual questions but more often opinions (sometimes dressed up as a question)? It doesn't matter whether the 'questioner' agrees or disagrees – people are compelled to tell you what they think. At the heart of those opinions are comparisons between what you just told them and what they know or think (or, again, think they know). They are presenting you with their assessment – a judgement.

Such workplace courses are often now run using facilitated discussion or activities to draw out learning points. The process starts with getting people to talk about what they already understand and to draw conclusions from their experience. New information can then be woven into the discussion along the way, better allowing people to assimilate new knowledge in the context of their existing experience. It's much less of a blunt instrument than a lecture, and it works with rather than against the knowledge and experience of those in the room.

> The dualistic mind moves toward resolution. It loves closure. It rushes toward judgement. That's why all great spiritual teachers said, 'Do not judge . . .' Now to us educated dualistic thinkers that just feels frankly irresponsible. We have to make judgements, don't we? And you do, but not at the first level. The first lens through which you receive the moment has to be non-dual, that I accept all parts: the good, that which

I understand; that which I don't understand, which might appear bad. And usually does. Most people don't go beyond that, I'm sorry to say. Anything that they yet don't understand is presumed to be wrong, dangerous, sinful, heretical or even to be destroyed. This is quite unfortunate.[5]

I remember as a boy a question that was sometimes asked by grown-ups in our church. It might be about a particular preacher or minister, a writer of theology or perhaps just somebody of influence in the Church. The question was: 'Is he sound?' (and it was generally 'he' then). How does he measure up to our benchmark of normal Christianity? Is he one of us? I grew up genuinely believing that my family was better than others because we were 'saved'. The particular bubble of Christianity I existed in didn't seem to pay much attention to Jesus' withering condemnation of the Pharisee at prayer who said, 'God, I thank you that I am not like other people' – demonstrating at a stroke that, actually, he was (Luke 18.11).

Being 'one of us' is a question that underpins much of the behaviour and politics in church life. Whether it is the soundness of your theology or simply if your face 'fits', judgementalism can be very subtly played out in church life. Approval is extended or withheld simply by the way you are included by your church: in whether or not you are asked to join a rota; approached to share in the Peace as fully as others; offered pastoral support or even just a cup of coffee; listed in the prayer diary; get to chat with the vicar at the door on the way out. It may not be overt or even consciously done. But if you are judged to be not one of us then our smiles may be a little less wide, the handshake more fleeting or, at our worst, we'll just ignore you and hope you go away.

All that, however, is the church playing out judgementalism in rather oblique ways. In other ways, Christians can be very clear about who must be separated out from the elite. I'm writing this during the summer in which the Church of England finally agreed to allow women to become bishops. For the legislation to pass Synod, arrangements had to be offered to those who adhere to a doctrine of 'male headship' – the view that ultimate authority can only rest with a man. Those churches will have an arrangement to come under the episcopal oversight of a male bishop.

He will, of course, also have to be heterosexual – or pretend to be. For the other great issue brewing in the Church of England is how it deals with gay clergy and bishops wishing to marry a partner of the same gender. Currently the Church judges homosexual clergy to be less than heterosexual, and enforces celibacy on those who are openly gay, who are also forbidden by canon law from entering into a same-sex marriage.

This kind of separating out is what the Levitical code of Moses did for the wandering people of Israel as they left slavery in Egypt in search of the promised land. In the course of their journey they would rub up against all sorts of other tribes with their own religions, customs, lifestyles and practices. In order to ensure Israel remained a distinct nation while it was in transit, a set of over 600 laws was issued to regulate their way of life.

> The mark of distinction between Israel and everyone else found most often in scripture is the distinction between clean and unclean. That is what the book of Leviticus is about: its catalogue of rules, including the fierce condemnation of sex between males, is a way to keep 'us' separate from 'them'.[6]

We don't, of course, follow the Levitical code any more. It was a set of rules for a particular people at a particular time. Christ came not only to fulfil that law but to enable Israel to realize her destiny in becoming a blessing to all nations (Genesis 22.18). Through him Israel becomes the cradle out of which salvation for all humanity is born. Hence the way we see Jesus' ministry beginning to include Gentiles, while the early Apostles push the point that there is to be no more separating out between the people who belong to Christ: no Jew or Greek, slave or free, male or female but all one in Christ Jesus (Galatians 3.28).

In a rather vivid experience, we see this breaking down of the things we do to judge ourselves as separate from others in Peter's striking vision in the Acts of the Apostles:

About noon the next day, as they were on their journey and approaching the city, Peter went up on the roof to pray. He became hungry and wanted something to eat; and while it was being prepared, he fell into a trance. He saw the heaven opened and something like a large sheet coming down, being lowered to the ground by its four corners. In it were all kinds of four-footed creatures and reptiles and birds of the air. Then he heard a voice saying, 'Get up, Peter; kill and eat.' But Peter said, 'By no means, Lord; for I have never eaten anything that is profane or unclean.' The voice said to him again, a second time, 'What God has made clean, you must not call profane.' This happened three times, and the thing was suddenly taken up to heaven.                    (Acts 10.9–16)

Peter is horrified at the suggestion that he should eat food that is forbidden because it is considered unclean. The incident occurs just as he is about to be called to the house of a Gentile who wants to hear the good news of Jesus Christ. At this point Peter realizes the point of his vision. The Jewish law that prevents him from associating with or visiting the home of a Gentile is at odds with the new-era kingdom of God that Jesus ushered in. 'God has shown me that I should not call anyone profane or unclean' (Acts 10.28). No more separating out, no more judging ourselves better than others, no more comparing ourselves more or less godly, purer or less defiled than others. It is an end to tribalism, to dualistic judgement. The barriers we erect between us are being broken down.

I think it is not insignificant that the focus of Peter's vision is on food. Sharing food together is a very special and socially binding experience. Family life finds its tightest expression around the meal table, perhaps the one time in the day when everyone comes together. Extending hospitality to guests begins with offering a drink or something to eat. Time spent with friends is focused on a cuppa, a meal or going out for a drink. Relationships are built and sustained through table fellowship.

So powerful is the act of eating together as a symbol of unity that in some places it is very purposefully used to segregate people, as Richard Cleaver recalls:

In the caste system in India, it is the test of one's standing in the hierarchy. Brahmans may accept food only from Brahmans; Kshatriyas, the next lower caste, only from Brahmans or Kshatriyas; and so on. I still remember laws [in the US] that prevented people of color eating with white people and drinking from the same water fountain.[7]

Today the Church uses its holiest meal to separate out those we deem not to be part of Jesus' in-crowd. We have institutionalized a form of judgementalism that is designed to assess whether you are good enough, clean enough, to be allowed to receive the sacrament. Haven't we moved a long way from the generous and inclusive table fellowship of Jesus Christ, who chose to dine with all the wrong people – those judged most unfit by society? The Church has become an elite who gatekeep the radical and inclusive love of God. It is as if we don't believe that the body of Christ, as expressed by both the sacrament and the community of people sharing it, has the power to heal or transform lives. Or maybe we do, but don't want just anybody getting their grubby hands on it.

In her book *Take This Bread*, Sara Miles recounts how she was converted to Christianity after wandering into a church one Sunday and receiving bread and wine that was freely offered to all. She didn't have a church upbringing, nor had she been baptized or confirmed, or screened for membership. She was simply a seeker. Her testimony is a reminder of the power of the body of Christ to transform people – not least when they are welcomed in with love and open arms to participate in Christ's abundant giving of himself. She writes about how, over the centuries, the Church evolved the Lord's Supper, losing much of its original meaning and intention along the way.

> Instead of being God's freely given gift of reconciliation for everyone – the central point of Jesus's barrier-breaking meals with sinners of all descriptions – communion belonged to the religious authorities.
>
> The entire contradictory package of Christianity was present in the Eucharist. A sign of unconditional acceptance and

forgiveness, it was doled out and rationed to insiders; a sign of unity, it divided people; a sign of the most common and ordinary human reality, it was rarefied and theorized nearly to death. And yet that meal remained, through all the centuries, more powerful than any attempts to manage it. It reconciled, if only for a minute, all of God's creation, revealing that, without exception, we were members of one body, God's body, in endless diversity. The feast showed us how to re-member what had been dis-membered by human attempts to separate and divide, judge and cast out, select or punish. At that Table, sharing food, we were brought into the ongoing work of making creation whole.[8]

Miles reminds us of the powerful symbolism of breaking bread together. The host is broken into pieces and distributed to those present. As we consume it the people become united as the body of Christ. Through something broken we are made whole – the divisions we create between ourselves fall away. But Christians have kneaded judgementalism into the Bread of Life, deciding who can and can't participate. In spite of this, the meal has survived and continues to be a powerful sacramental moment for millions of Christians around the world. It transcends the lowest-common-denominator humanity that we bring to Christ's table and, in spite of ourselves, God's grace trumps our addiction to judgementalism and retains the power to heal it.

Thankfully voices like Sara Miles' are being increasingly heard within the mainstream Church. And we do need them. In an age when our faith is under pressure from falling attendance while on the receiving end of the caustic judgementalism of secular sceptics, there has never been a more important time for Christianity to rediscover its radically inclusive roots and rise above the human instinct for tribalism from which Christ wishes to redeem us.

However much or little we judge those around us in comparison with ourselves, one thing is clear: it is simply not how God operates. The kind of dualistic judgementalism humans engage in is not part of the divine operating system – 'he makes his sun rise on the evil and on the good, and sends rain on the righteous and on the unrighteous' (Matthew 5.45). It is scandalous to human minds that God should love everyone equally. Religion often struggles to cope with this and finds ways to build faith on a foundation of self-righteousness and condemnation of others.

As we'll see later, that was an issue that would particularly vex Jesus. His challenge to the judgementalism of the religious elite would make him some very powerful enemies.

# 3

## *Fear*

———•◆•———

The roots of judgementalism go deeper than an unwillingness to embrace difference or a compulsion to determine whether or not we're better than the next person. The anxiety triggered by the approaching stranger prompts us to ask, 'Is this person a friend or an enemy?' Or to put it another way, 'Should I be afraid?'

Fear is hardwired into the human psyche and is a profoundly important driver in the decisions we make and the way we choose to live our lives. Perhaps the only difference in the role of fear between primitive times and today is the ever more sophisticated ways others have learnt to exploit our fears to get us to do what they want.

Trading in fear has become one of the commodities of modern life. Politicians play to our fears when they develop manifestos and canvas our votes. Horror is a popular and lucrative genre of both literature and cinema. Sometimes we like to flirt with the fear that comes from a terror ride in an amusement park, bungee jumping or white-water rafting.

The media have learnt that fear – like sex – sells. The sheer volume of scaremongering headlines is testament to how effectively they shift papers off the news stands. One enterprising teenager got so sick of the endless scare stories about cancer in his mother's tabloid that he posted a list of them on the internet. He documented almost 150 supposed causes of cancer reported by that one paper over several years. These included such unlikely carcinogens as flip-flops, till receipts and hugging. It truly is a scary world out there![1]

Learning to handle our fears is certainly not a new aspect of living but the manipulation of them in modern times has arguably reached unprecedented levels – this in spite of our living in a safer society than at any time in history. In his book *Following Jesus in a Culture of Fear*, Scott Bader-Saye outlines many of the ways our fears are being manipulated by those with a vested interest in doing so.

> Politicians, the media, advertisers, even religious leaders, have a profit motive for exacerbating and sustaining our fears. This profit may come in the form of money, viewership, filled pews, influence, or power, but in each case we are encouraged to fear the wrong things or to fear the right things in the wrong way. Our anxiety, then, drives us to act in ways that override other moral concerns. We spend our money based on fear rather than stewardship. We make political decisions based on fear rather than the common good. We participate in religious life based on fear rather than love.[2]

Bader-Saye goes on to discuss the impact of fear on the Christian imperative to reach out in love to those around us. Fear causes us to withdraw into ourselves and becomes an impediment to offering hospitality, generosity and friendship.

Some 800 years ago, when Europe was a far bloodier and more precarious place to live than today, Thomas Aquinas described the way fear causes 'a certain contraction in the appetite', with the result that we 'extend' ourselves to 'fewer things'.[3] It is another instinct that causes us to separate ourselves out from others. One of the great challenges of inner-city parish ministry is getting past the way people insulate themselves and their lives from others. Gated communities, controlled access to social housing and a dwindling use of public spaces like pubs, community halls and churches makes the work of reaching out to others very much harder. In the streets and on public transport, we isolate ourselves with our smartphones, MP3 players and newspapers.

It was somewhat refreshing to encounter the residents of a housing estate in Hackney in east London who lobbied against council plans to fence in their estate to 'help them feel safer'. The tenants association recognized that by sealing themselves off from the rest of the neighbourhood it would inhibit the social integration they had worked hard to build. I have a suspicion the rise of controlled access to living spaces intensifies fear and distrust of the outside world, and that the sense of safety enjoyed within is relative to the exaggerated fears the presence of security measures provoke in the first place.

To judge others a threat causes the same impulse we looked at earlier, in which we separate ourselves off to create an existence with ourselves at the centre. This is a big problem for Christians for whom the notion of *making me the centre of my life* is, in Scripture, given a very powerful word – sin. Too often reduced to the idea of breaking the rules, sin has a much broader and richer meaning, describing the instinct to focus in on ourself instead of trusting in God.

But fear inhibits trust, while sin leads us to pull up the drawbridge and prime the battlements with ammunition, ready to challenge any who threaten our sense of stability, safety or status quo.

'The path out of fear is not power but trust, not strength but vulnerability before God', says Bader-Saye.[4] The quest for those of us who seek the way of the cross is surely to relocate a trust in God at the heart of our existence in such a way that it dislodges the primal urge to repel anyone who rocks our boat.

So many of the worst things in human history have been driven by fear. Today the fears that are spread through the media about Islam are fuelling a resurgence of the far right in Europe. Many are not even conscious of the way the press are forming their anti-Islam anxieties.

In an illuminating exercise for a television documentary, the political journalist Peter Oborne showed newspaper headlines to members of the public to test their reactions. Each headline said something about 'Jews' or 'Blacks'. People were shocked that the press today were allowed to publish such blatant anti-Semitic and racist stories. But the headlines had been doctored by Oborne. He then turned the cards over to show the actual headlines, which were exactly the same – except that in place of 'Jews' or 'Blacks' were the words 'Muslims' or 'Islam'. The drip, drip, drip of derogatory messages fed to us by the press about Muslims, asylum seekers, benefit claimants or whoever the latest target is begin to shape a consciousness founded on fear. And soon we judge all Muslims (peace-loving or terrorist), all asylum seekers (tortured or merely frightened), all benefit claimants (responsible or reckless) to be the same.

Much of this fearfulness comes from feeling that our sense of who we are is challenged by different ideas, traditions or customs that others might introduce into our society. We might not remain who we are if other people start turning up and doing things differently.

The Church certainly bears that hallmark in its culture. For many, church is a place where they seek something constant in a world of fast-paced change. I think it is too. But that *something* is God, not the hymns we sing, the prayer book we use, how we organize the jumble sale, the size of the poster on the railings or who gets to arrange the flowers. A colleague emailed me last week to say how he was getting on in his new parish. 'The best way of looking at it,' he writes, 'is that at least my people are passionate about things. That means banging fists on tables etc.' Many incumbents new to a parish have to put up with shouting, sulking, storming out and more subtle passive-aggressive behaviours over what seem the most trivial things. Fear of change among those who need to hold on to something unchanging explains a lot of bad behaviour in church life, including judgementalism. But we cling to the wrong things.

The theologian James Alison sees something of this fearfulness in the trauma caused to many Christians by changing attitudes to homosexuality:

> I rather suspect that the issue of gay love and relationships, really rather unimportant and banal in itself, has become a sort of hermeneutical flash point because those who find the 'natural' order of the world and of their own lives gradually melting away beneath them under the pressure of an ever more obviously socially constructed world – and that means one for which we are invited to take responsibility – are flailing about trying to establish an order outside themselves. A crisis of identity needs someone else to be responsible for it so that they can be sacrificed and decent order and stability established, which of course it never really is.[5]

I see something like this in the conversations I have around the parish about new thinking on many subjects, where fear of change causes psychological alarm. Just think for example about how often you hear – or perhaps speak – the words, 'It's political correctness gone mad.' Attempts to change the social norms and certainties we grew up with cause a kind of psychological stress. The reflex is to reject the suggestion, and possibly also the person arguing for a new point of view.

Much of the heat under our collars isn't actually about homosexuality, immigrants, urban regeneration, new liturgy or the best way to talk about disabled people. It's an internal instability caused by something unfamiliar. Thankfully humans have the ability, if they choose, to pause and take stock when presented with something new, to get acquainted with it, examine it from all sides and come to a discerning view. But we have to choose to make that happen. If we simply rely on our gut feeling then we aren't thinking at all and are more likely to make harsh judgements that reject new ideas and those who present them.

When I see fringe politicians who want to isolate the country, restore traditional values (whose tradition?), stop immigration or cut foreign aid budgets, I see people who are characterized not by a vision of the common good but powerfully compelled by their own fear. And why wouldn't they feel afraid? If you have nothing permanent or unchanging in your life to anchor you, then of course you're left flailing about trying to find an alternative.

Christians do have such an anchor, as found in our relationship with God. In the words of Priscilla J. Owens' nineteenth-century American hymn:

> We have an anchor that keeps the soul
> Steadfast and sure while the billows roll,
> Fastened to the Rock which cannot move,
> Grounded firm and deep in the Savior's love.[6]

But so powerful is the fear instinct within us that it's easy to lose a grip on our hope in God and cast around for something else to hang on to. For many of us, not just loony politicians but in church life too, that thing is *the past*. Particularly, perhaps, for those with a stable upbringing, the past can have a powerful and alluring hold. But it's also an utterly unreliable one. As someone once put it, 'The past is never where you think you left it.'[7] Our memories can be remarkably unreliable, and while misty-eyed nostalgia might induce a warm and comforting feeling, it makes a very unstable foundation for, well, pretty much anything – unless you're in the cupcake business, or are Cath Kidston.

While God may be unchanging, theological thinking evolves. The span of Scripture, written over a few thousand years, tells the story of how the children of Abraham understood God; how that thinking evolved and deepened under the influence of Moses, judges, kings and prophets; how Jesus came and cast new light on that understanding and heralded a new era of the emerging kingdom of God; how the early Church grappled with the implications of Christ's teaching, personal example, death and resurrection, and then took the good news to people who did not have Judaism as a common base upon which to build their faith. God is fundamentally the same but understood rather differently by the end of the New Testament compared to the start of the Hebrew Scriptures. And that deepening of understanding has continued through 2,000 years of theological study, biblical scholarship and the journey of God's people through history.

God is a paradox that is both unfathomable while also capable of, and desiring to be, in relationship with us. No wonder the Church squabbles like mad with itself. We are still trying to grasp hold of something beyond our full comprehension. I hang on to Christ because I can at least get my head in part around what he helps us know about God's nature and how to respond to it. But even his teaching is super-challenging to human nature.

Faith can be a turbulent ride, and there's nothing in the Gospels to suggest it should be otherwise. Jesus hints, more than once, at the divisiveness that following him will bring to our relationships with one another. He warns us to expect this. He didn't present neat answers on a plate to his disciples but leaves them scratching their heads at his opaque parables. They're left to wrestle with his teaching, much as we do today. That's the deal I'm afraid. Those who claim they completely know God and have it all worked out are false prophets – and Jesus foresaw plenty of those too. No: this kingdom business is a bit tricky to grasp.

It's understandable, then, that Christians sometimes fixate on elements of church life that must be set in stone – the form of the liturgy, points of order in committee meetings, the type of lace on a priest's vestments, the secret recipe for non-alcoholic communion wine, what people can do in bed with each other without making the Holy Spirit blush. None of which much suggests that we feel at ease with ourselves or secure in our relationships with God. I'm not saying nothing matters but I am clear that if we really got what the gospel is about then we wouldn't get so vexed or be so horrible to our brothers and sisters in Christ. Like children who fight each other for their parents' approval, judgementalism in church life is a mark of our insecurity. Jesus, himself the focus of religious fear, laments for us.

> Jerusalem, Jerusalem, the city that kills the prophets and stones those who are sent to it! How often have I desired to gather your children together as a hen gathers her brood under her wings, and you were not willing! (Luke 13.34)

Jesus' message of God's love and the radical egalitarianism of God's kingdom posed such a threat to the pious religiosity of the temple elite that they responded the way we often do to those whose ideas threaten our security – they rejected him, and his message, out of hand. They put Jesus to death just to make sure they really shut him up. The trouble with a good idea, and certainly with the truth, is that it has a nasty habit of bubbling up again. It won't be held down. Tempting as it may be to see the resurrection as a great 'ta-dah!' moment ('That'll teach you, suckers'), it really speaks of the futility of trying to tame God for our own ends or to control others' beliefs so that we can stay nicely tucked up in our comfort zone. We might try this on with each other but, when it comes to God, God's way will wriggle itself out of our control-freakery and make itself known. That's why moral support for slavery by the Church eventually crumbled. It's why ecclesiastical subjugation of women is collapsing. It's why the emerging Church is brushing off the stifling accretion of respectable church culture and rediscovering vibrant worship and mission. It's why you might even find an LGBT minister in the pulpit.

We have a long way to go, and mastering our fears about change is fundamental to our ability to trust in God. The Church is ever changing, evolving and adapting – albeit with frustrating slowness. Each generation has to wrestle with the challenges of its day and work out how God's word speaks into that situation. The Holy Spirit is a lithe and creative force. She doesn't seek to spray the Church in quick-drying cement so that we set fast and are ever thus. She is Christ's gift to the Church to help us recover ancient truth in modern times. Change is in the small print of faith. If that makes you feel wobbly inside, that's only natural. But when we find ourselves unable to engage with the new and clinging to the status quo, it's time to hit the hassock with our knees and listen hard for the voice of the Spirit as she whispers to us, 'Trust in God.'

Or as the first epistle of John puts it, 'perfect love casts out fear' (1 John 4.18).

# 4

## *Blame and scapegoating*

Fear isn't the only psychological commodity in heavy use by the media today. It's fairly evenly matched by another bedfellow of judgementalism – blame. When a news story blows up about an accident, act of violence or political scandal (even, oddly, a natural disaster), a question that will be picked over forensically by the media for days and weeks to come is, 'Who is to blame?'

I'm all for people taking responsibility for their actions or trusted public servants being called to account. But blame has become a modern obsession. The ever more litigious nature of our society, egged on by ambulance-chasing lawyers, means the range of things held to be somebody's fault has grown ever larger – often fuelled by the dismal hope that somewhere along the line there might be financial compensation; as if a wodge of cash will put everything right.

One of the woeful things about running a church these days is the burden of health-and-safety practices, risk assessments, safe-guarding procedures and criminal-record checks we have to imple-ment. There are good reasons why some of these are now in place but they can be a source of constant worry about covering your back when trying to do the most innocuous things. It sometimes feels as though you can't hold a Bible study without dreading that someone will flick through their Bible too fast . . . inflicting a paper cut on their finger . . . which then turns septic and drops off . . . all because they weren't wearing safety gloves . . . Because if that did happen, *it would be all my fault!*

You don't have to spend very much time in this kind of climate before every good idea you have about mission and ministry becomes undermined by anticipating all the things that might go wrong or the time and money you'd have to expend on eliminating all risks. Blame is a very noxious element to have floating around us all the time. More than anything, perhaps, it encourages us to view others as the cause of any misfortune that befalls us. It ignores personal responsibility and denies what's always been a truism in life – bad stuff happens.

If I collude with this tendency to blame others, it stops me being truthful about myself. Rather than reflecting honestly on my circumstances and my own contribution in shaping them, blame assumes my innocence and casts others as the authors of my misfortune. There isn't much self-awareness or integrity here. Nor is there room to grow. Indeed a blame mentality is pretty certain to stunt my growth towards holiness.

At the same time it casts others as the villain of the piece, nurturing a judgemental attitude that's magnificently self-righteous. I've done a bit of reconciliation work in the past, where colleagues have fallen out and their ability to work together has been damaged. In every case where a resolution occurred it was because both parties were big enough to abandon blame and be honest about themselves and each other. Invariably they would understand how they'd both contributed to their situation. It's at the point where disagreement turns into blame and self-justification that positions become entrenched and recovery of a working relationship very hard. In cases where attempts at reconciliation failed, it was due to one party being unable or unwilling to get past blaming the other.

I can certainly think back to situations where I've refused to move beyond blaming others. It's a sort of attempt at punishing them, and one's internal dialogue becomes full of judgement towards them. A kind of stubbornness sets in, which ultimately only imprisons and isolates us.

So blame is a very nasty social commodity, but there is now so much of it swirling around us in society that it's become normalized. Political life and the adversarial nature of Parliament seem to have turned into a ping-pong of blame – getting at the truth seems less important than landing a blow on the other side. The media stokes the flames of this, not only giving a platform to politicians to have a go at each other but also turning on them periodically, blaming them for the country's problems. Jim Wallis, writing about media coverage of politics in the USA, says:

> The 24/7 news coverage today, especially on radio, cable, and the internet blogosphere, doesn't really 'cover' the news but rather fuels the audience's already-held prejudices about what is happening. Almost all of it is biased, much of it is distorted, some of it is just plain lies, and too much of it is downright hateful. Unfortunately, we are losing genuinely important ideas that the other political side has, which are often critically needed to find more balanced answers to our complex social, political, and economic problems. We've lost our *integrity* in the public arena, substituting ideological warfare for genuine and rigorous political debate, replacing substance with sound bites . . . In such a polarized, paralyzed, and increasingly poisonous political environment, it is very difficult to find or even discuss the common good.[1]

In the blame and judgement game, we lose the capacity to work together effectively or to generate creative new ideas to solve our problems. I'm reminded of the prayer, 'Redeem our national life so that we cease to promote hatred, dishonesty and violence.'[2]

A few years ago a planning application was submitted to the local authority to turn a building near our church into a hostel for homeless people. A good deal of opposition to this built up in the local community, on the grounds that a bunch of vagrants loitering around the neighbourhood would lead to an increase in street crime – already an issue in the neighbourhood. No evidence was presented that demonstrated a link between homelessness and crime. In fact we argued that people would be less likely to offend once they're in accommodation with some of their basic needs taken care of, rather than in the desperate hand-to-mouth existence of sleeping rough.

There was a lot going on in this situation: a prejudice against homeless people presumed responsible for their own misfortune; snobbishness about the tone of the neighbourhood being lowered by the arrival of people who were not middle-class professionals;

fear about protecting property; scapegoating a category of people for a pre-existing problem of petty crime.

A number of ancient cultures adopted scapegoating as a means of shifting blame for their misfortunes or bad behaviour. The people of Israel, wandering the desert following their exodus from slavery in Egypt, would cast out a goat as a means of atonement, to wander off into the wilderness and die, the poor animal symbolically bearing away the sins of the community (Leviticus 16.7–10). The ancient Greeks would respond to calamity by ejecting a prisoner or disabled person from the community. The anti-Semitic policies of Nazi Germany led to an entire ethno-religious group being blamed for the country's problems. Closer to home, whole categories of people have in some minds become scapegoats for the problems of the country today – immigrants, bankers, the EU, Muslims, politicians. Scapegoating is a vehicle that travels quickly between blame and prejudice.

In our day-to-day judgementalism of others there is a subtler form of scapegoating at work, which psychologists call *projection*. As I've mentioned, I get very annoyed when other people are judgemental. Internally what's going on is that I know that I too am far too quick to judge others. I know it, and I certainly don't like it. As I'm so good at pointing the finger I can readily spot the same behaviour in those around me. My mind copes with the burden of loathing and darkness I feel about my own judgemental trait by getting vexed when I see it in others. I project my dislike onto others as an – albeit momentary – means of soothing myself, so I can feel angry or hateful about them rather than directing it inwards. It's a psychological defence mechanism.

Perhaps you can think of a time when you have judged others on their behaviour or their looks and later realized that what bothered you was really something about yourself that you saw in them. 'He is such a gossip', we might say; 'Look at the bum on her!'; 'What a snob!'; 'He just never listens.'

Thomas Merton wrote:

It is not only our hatred of others that is dangerous but also and above all our hatred of ourselves: particularly that hatred of ourselves which is too deep and too powerful to be consciously faced. For it is this which makes us see our own evil in others and unable to see it in ourselves.[3]

Mahatma Gandhi said, 'The impurity of my associates is but the manifestation of the hidden wrong within me.'[4]

This idea that our own shortcomings are mirrored in those around us casts a new light on Christ's instruction to forgive others with abundance and generosity.

> Peter came and said to him, 'Lord, if another member of the church sins against me, how often should I forgive? As many as seven times?' Jesus said to him, 'Not seven times, but, I tell you, seventy-seven times.' (Matthew 18.21–22)

When we are able to come to terms with the failings of others we become better at forgiving ourselves. When we consciously open up the darker parts of our psyche to the love of God, our need to project our self-judgement onto others diminishes.

Inner and outer worlds are deeply entwined when it comes to judgementalism. We saw earlier how fear causes us to withdraw into ourselves; that in failing to trust God we allow anxieties rather than faith to become the heart of our existence; that judging others is a form of self-justification that splits us off from others in a delusion of our own normality. Now we are also beginning to see how the spiritual task is a right ordering of the inner life, which in turn has an impact on our visible and outward behaviour. Projecting our dislike of our own traits onto another leads us to judgement and blame: self-examination is replaced by setting others straight. This will never lead to healing. The link between forgiving others and healing our own inner pain is a kind of justice, which reflects the divine who 'does justice by restoring things instead of punishing them'.[5]

In his book *Dark Nights of the Soul*, Thomas Moore suggests we reimagine scapegoating, 'not as finding someone to blame but uncovering the spirit in all of us that is the source of the evil in the world'.[6]

To do so requires a willingness to yield to the reality that we all have a shadow side, which we largely try to hide from others.

One of the ways we pretend we don't have any dark thoughts or feelings is to demonize those we think do. The dishonesty inherent in cloaking our true selves with respectability inevitably leads to seeing oneself as better than others, which is a denial of the reality of the darkness within.

A fully rounded spirituality neither pretends there is no shadow side nor tries to get rid of it. Rather we open it up and let God in. It is a way of offering the whole of ourselves to Christ who, lest we forget, already knows all about our shadow side. He can't be conned.

Moore invites us to see all that is wrong in the world and in the behaviour of others as present within our own shadow side. This kind of grounded honesty offers a very different starting point in our relationship with others – I am like you. The need to compare ourselves as better or worse than others collapses as we recognize we are in the same boat – all have sinned and fall short of the glory of God.

This is hard when we are a little bit afraid of our own darkness. At our most honest we know that much of what we see in others – even in the most appalling atrocities – is only an extension of the same impulses that drive us: fear, the need to control, the desire for power, the hunger to be better than others, an inability to cope with difference in those around us.

And these are sinful impulses, in that they always centre on our self. While we may sometimes be afraid of them, God is utterly and completely not so. Christ has already done the work that conquers evil, so we need not fear it whether in ourselves or the actions of others. In the risen life of Christ we see the promise of new life for us, which is ours to claim, freely given through God's grace. It doesn't mean we become perfect overnight, but it does mean we can set out on the road to wholeness, being honest about our own dark side and setting aside fear, blame and judgement when we observe them in others.

# 5

## Pride and ignorance

How is it that people who are quite obviously eaten up with Pride can say they believe in God and appear to themselves very religious? I am afraid it means they are worshipping an imaginary God. They theoretically admit themselves to be nothing in the presence of this phantom God, but are really all the time imagining how He approves of them and thinks them far better than ordinary people ... Whenever we find that our religious life is making us feel that we are good – above all, that we are better than someone else – I think we may be sure that we are being acted on, not by God, but by the devil.
C. S. Lewis[1]

Pride is a particular human quality that, in its worst manifestation, shows itself in a capacity to be really quite pleased with ourselves. Pride doesn't only lead us into the kind of dualistic comparisons that help us judge ourselves better than others (which is certainly bad enough), it also acts as a barrier to God's work in us.

In 2 Kings 5 we read the story of Naaman, an army commander, who contracted a skin disease. He is told by a captured slave girl in his household that a prophet from her homeland will be able to heal him. That he listens to the advice of a slave, a girl and a foreigner suggests he must be *really* desperate to find a cure.

Naaman goes to visit Elisha, who refuses to speak to him but sends a messenger telling Naaman to wash in the river Jordan seven times and he will be healed. Naaman is offended, in part because Elisha won't even bother to see him face to face. A man used to commanding an army is not accustomed to being treated in such an offhand manner. The offence is compounded by the cure on offer: Elisha's solution has none of the liturgical protocol Naaman expected. What kind of cure involves multiple baths in a notoriously filthy river? With his pride injured and his mind on critical red alert, Naaman storms off in a thumping great huff.

Naaman's judgementalism creates a substantial hindrance to God's work in his life. At the root of that judgement is his pride (dented) and the assumptions (superficial) that he makes about Elisha and the means through which God will work to heal him. It takes a faithful servant to talk him round. 'Father, if the prophet had commanded you to do something difficult, would you not have done it? How much more, when all he said to you was, "Wash, and be clean"?' (2 Kings 5.13).

Naaman finally consents and, as Elisha foretold, is completely cured of his skin complaint. I find it easy to identify with Naaman's behaviour in this situation, thinking of times my initial encounter with others has led me to judge their whole character in a bad light based on that one moment. I recall other times when I've closed down the opportunities a situation might have offered me because it didn't fulfil my initial expectations (the number of conferences I have left half way through the day, for example, only to hear from others that the best bit was in the afternoon – d'oh!).

And how often has pride fuelled my judgementalism? Those times when a fragile ego has tried to console itself by lashing out at someone else? It isn't simply the case that we make ourselves feel better by diminishing others, as discussed earlier. Much judgementalism sets out to shore up gratifying feelings of superiority – which is, of course, a benchmark for nothing at all. The gift wrap may be different but the underlying behaviour is still driven by self-obsession.

St Augustine wrote: 'In proportion as our inflated egos are healed of their pride, we become more full of love. And with what is a person full who is full of love, if not with God?'[2]

Well that sounds just super, Gus, but blimey: isn't it hard to adopt the kind of humility that seeks the path of love rather than playing the game of keeping up appearances? And church life is so often dominated by thrusting egos and clashing horns, locked in a struggle of domination with Phyllis on who gets to starch the altar linen or Bob on how best to programme the boiler.

There are often people who not only contribute magnificently to church life but endlessly blow their own trumpets to make sure everyone knows it. Or they complain about what a burden it is to buy the milk for after-church coffee every week, when nobody shows any appreciation. And yet, strangely, all offers of help are rebuffed. They don't actually want anyone to intrude on their role, they just want everyone to know how essential they are (and, to be fair, we could often be a lot better at showing appreciation and not taking people for granted). But I'm sure you'll have encountered people whose participation in church is not so much driven by a spirit of joyful service as one of dismal self-importance that fails to see others fully.

As Francis de Sales writes: 'Some judge rashly out of pride: they pull others down because they need to push themselves up.'[3] The fullness of self that is evident in pride stands in contrast to the self-emptying humility Christ demonstrates. We build a very wobbly platform for ourselves when we dispense judgement towards others rooted in our own pride.

There is a type of Christian for whom spiritual pride is de rigueur, where feeling rather pleased with oneself for being saved leads to pity and judgement towards those they deem outside Christ's salvific action. I know such people exist because I used to be one, and we felt really pleased with ourselves. Clever old us for doing the right thing and opening up our hearts to Jesus – and stupid old you if you don't do the same, because one day it will be too late and then you'll be sorry.

In the UK there's a sign painted on the side of a lorry parked in a field somewhere off the great north–south A1 highway. It says, 'Prepare to meet your God. Believe in the Lord Jesus Christ and you will be saved.' This isn't exactly off-message, but the approach to communicating the good news of the gospel is not very Christlike. His message was delivered as an invitation and a promise: 'The kingdom of God is at hand.' There isn't very much invitational about threatening people into conversion and proclaiming that you possess the truth and everyone else better buy into it or are for the high jump. Can you see where pride might be at the root of this approach?

'If your heart is gentle, your judgements will be gentle; if it is loving, so will your judgements be. Rash judgement leads to contempt, pride and complacency, and many other evils.'[4] He may have been writing in the seventeenth century, but here Francis de Sales nails it for modern times.

A more recent writer, Cynthia Bourgeault, puts it this way:

Unlike the egoic operating system [Bourgeault's term for dualistic thinking], the heart does not perceive through differentiation. It doesn't divide the field into inside and out, subject and object. Rather, it perceives by means of harmony . . . When heart-awareness becomes fully formed within a person, he or she will be operating out of nondual consciousness. But it's not simply a higher level of the same old mind; it's a whole new operating system! That person does indeed see from a perspective of singleness – and just as Jesus called for, there is now no separation between God and humans, or between humans and other humans, simply because separation isn't factored into the new operating system. It is no longer necessary for perception, so it simply falls away like scales from the eyes.[5]

The problem with being full of oneself, with using *me* as a benchmark for others, is that I'm not conscious of my own blind spots or lack of knowledge. The rush to judge does not allow time to gather all the facts.

A few years ago a story appeared in the press about a Chinese baby rescued from a toilet waste pipe. Condemnation was swift for the person who would do such a heartless thing. We were reminded of the stiff fines there are for Chinese parents who have more than one child, suggesting this as a motive for trying to flush a baby away. Charges for attempted murder would be sure to follow. From a single piece of information about the remarkable rescue, a whole judgemental narrative was woven together by the media.

Information emerged the following day that put the story in a very different light. A young woman had given birth unexpectedly while using the toilet. Unable to retrieve the newborn herself she had raised the alarm and called the rescue services, remaining present throughout the recovery operation. After some treatment in hospital the baby was later reunited with her mother. An outpouring of sympathy followed.

Judgementalism forms a view about a person's motivation or character without collecting enough information first. It's so easy to make sweeping judgements about others in everyday life. For example, when we brand someone as 'lazy', what does this actually mean? A manager who decides a colleague is lazy is making an entirely subjective judgement about that person, and doing so in a way that won't help move the situation forward – the manager simply dismisses the colleague as flawed. The concept of laziness is a dead end.

As I've written elsewhere, if you reframe the problem and ask, 'Why is this person avoiding work?' then the way ahead opens up. Once you can identify an underlying cause, you're beginning to think more constructively about how to help someone overcome avoidance. And there may be very good reasons for that avoidance: stress, tiredness, anxiety, lack of confidence, distractions, lack of support, time or resources, fear of criticism and so on.[6]

But that's a lot of work. Much easier simply to write the colleague off than spend all that time trying to understand the person or situation and think constructively about it. Ironically, to brand someone as lazy is in itself a rather lazy thing to do. The truth is that many of us would rather stay in the comfort zone of our own ignorance than extend ourselves to understanding others.

Part of that understanding is to accept that, like ourselves, everyone else is flawed. When we stop pretending we're perfect, as well as avoiding placing others on a pedestal (from which they will one day surely topple), we can begin to reach an accommodation with others' shortcomings. As Thomas Merton wrote:

In our refusal to accept the partially good intentions of others and work with them (of course prudently and with resignation to the inevitable imperfection of the result) we are unconsciously proclaiming our own malice, our own intolerance, our own lack of realism, our own ethical and political quackery.[7]

Our own ethical quackery – what a tremendous way of putting it. Merton encourages us to recognize that any joint enterprise with others will be imperfect. The people it's easiest to work alongside are those most at ease with this reality. It's the ones who expect perfection, are unforgiving about the shortcomings of those around them, sneer and backbite and are constantly critical who are hard to be around. And from my own personal experience of being like that at times, it's an exhausting and highly unsatisfactory state in which to exist.

Merton's point is that we should discern the good intentions that lie behind the behaviour of those around us. This is similar to Desmond Tutu's view that we're made for goodness. As creatures made in the image of God, we're essentially good and have the capacity to reflect the divine when we learn to master ourselves. Whatever else sin might mean, it doesn't indicate that we're bad to our core – although you'll certainly hear that preached in plenty of churches. Our flaws overlay the goodness at our core, and the human journey is one of seeking to fulfil our potential for goodness.

The Quaker view that 'There is that of God in everyone' reminds us to look for the goodness in others rather than seeking out their flaws. It is in setting aside our pride that we're better able to see the good in others, even when their attempts to exercise that goodness are ham-fisted, short-sighted, self-centred or crass. That's the brokenness of their humanity showing itself. We don't need to worry about that either, because Christ has taken care of it. I'm not suggesting we should be naive about others – prudence and discernment are also qualities we must cultivate, as we'll see later.

But in opting to exercise our ability to see beyond the surface or the face people choose to present to us, we rein in our tendency for rash judgement and take the time to seek a fuller understanding.

While we're on the subject of blind spots, we should mention social norms – those aspects of public and cultural acceptability we all take for granted. One of the gifts of living in a diverse and increasingly tolerant society is that there's room for norms to be questioned or challenged. It was once the norm to thrash children, jail homosexuals and fire women from jobs when they married. When the majority of people inherit and sustain a social norm it becomes taken for granted, normal. We often join in with the norms of our time unthinkingly. Periodically there's a step shift in collective thinking that readjusts what we believe to be acceptable – except for traditionalists who like to tell us the old ways are best.

We look back, often scornfully, at times when punishments were harsh for trivial offences or people were ostracized for being left-handed or Irish. But we need to remain vigilant to those norms of our own day that future generations will look back on in disbelief, to listen to the outriders of new ideas who challenge the received opinions of the day.

The concept of 'political correctness' does much to harm our capacity to check ourselves. Invariably used pejoratively against those who challenge social norms, the charge of political correctness is dismissive of attempts to examine our collective blind spots and rethink the way society talks about or engages with particular issues. When we say 'That's political correctness gone mad', we're really saying, 'I'm not prepared to stop and consider what insight this person might have to offer.' It is another way of proclaiming our ethical and political quackery.

Today's political correctness often becomes tomorrow's social norm, so it's worth giving thought to it – none of which is to suggest that it doesn't sometimes indeed go mad. But how can we discern wisely if we rashly dismiss it before taking time to engage with it with a curious and open mind? To label something as politically correct is to make a judgement about it, and like so many judgements, it shuts down new possibilities that might actually be life enhancing.

The offhand dismissiveness with which some of us greet a new idea occurs because our own personal experience has such a grip on us. Someone once described the memory as being like a jelly: every experience we have is like a drip of boiling water landing on the jelly, corroding a small dimple on its surface. Every experience of the same kind lands another hot drip on exactly the same part of the jelly, creating ever deeper impressions. Soon the surface of the mind is covered in lots of dimples – some larger, some smaller – that bear testimony to the life we've lived.

These impressions condition our world view. Clearly, experiences we haven't had leave no impression, so we can't take these into account in the judgements we make. The way the subconscious mind works is to respond to new situations and ideas with the data collected from past experiences. The deeper the impression a repeated experience has on us, the more we're inclined to consider that to be *normal*. The arrival of something new outside our experience challenges the way we see the world.

If you've spent your entire life eating meat twice a day, one's first encounter with passionate vegetarians may seem quite odd. You might even consider them a bit cuckoo. Once you've encountered several more vegetarians then you might, should you choose to open your mind a bit, come to realize that it isn't that strange and is simply some people's personal choice. It doesn't reflect in any way on their state of mind, reliability, sociability or all-round niceness. But on that first encounter the subconscious mind will likely wave a red flag at you and shout 'weirdo!' And once the mind is on weirdo alert, our inclination is to back off, be dismissive or execute a rash judgement.

Vegetarianism, of course, isn't at all strange or exotic these days. But society continues to offer up ever wider and more interesting varieties of people and beliefs. Seeing women undertake jobs previously only ever done by men can cause us, at the very least, to do a double-take. We know there's no reason why a woman shouldn't, say, drive a bus or a taxi, but if you've only ever experienced men in those roles the first encounter makes an impression. Some people will doubtless take time to adjust to seeing a woman as a bishop, but we know from the ordination of women to the

Anglican priesthood – and in ministry in other denominations long before that – that it will soon become unremarkable for all but a minority. But what if we were to install a post-op transsexual bishop? If that's a strange idea to you, or you're not even sure what it means, I hope your first response would be, 'I need to know more so that I can understand the issues better and come to an informed view', rather than 'It's political correctness gone mad!'

We jump to conclusions – and not always the right ones – when we unthinkingly allow past and limited experience to inform our view of new ideas or situations.

When the prophet Samuel visited Jesse to anoint one of his sons as king, Jesse wheeled out all his big strapping macho boys one by one – only to have them rejected as not of God's choosing (1 Samuel 16.1–13). It's only when the youngest, David, is brought in from the fields where he's been shepherding that God is satisfied. We learn that God doesn't judge people, as we do, by outward appearance, but by the heart – although to be honest I've always felt the power of this narrative is rather undermined when it transpires David is something of a dreamboat: 'ruddy . . . beautiful eyes . . . handsome' (v. 12). Ding-dong! Whatever they imagined a king to look like (probably a grown man rather than a lad), David wasn't it. But God has other ideas.

Giving God room to work in our lives and our society means checking ourselves from jumping to conclusions or rushing in with snap judgements. It requires a particular kind of humility (which we will explore in more detail later), grounded in the reality of who we are, with all our blind spots, limited experience, hang-ups and ignorance. To get to that point necessitates an uncoupling from our own pride and self-satisfaction and really asking ourselves: 'Who are we to judge?'

# 6

## *Shame and self-judgement*

———•·•·•———

Our experiences in life don't merely inform our judgements and opinions. They can shape our whole psychological outlook. Nowhere is this more evident than the toxic effect of feeling shame.

Children who grow up in the shadow of a favoured sibling, don't fulfil their parents' expectations or whose early emotional life is not supported properly – or who are in some other way not accepted – learn that in order to be loved they must be someone else. If, for example, you grow up gay in a conservative environment you certainly learn that your true self is an abhorrence.

Shame inhibits us from full self-acceptance, and people develop different coping strategies to manage the feelings of self-loathing or inadequacy that have taken root. One of these is being judgemental towards others, but has its foundation in the judgements we direct at ourselves. The clinical psychologist Alan Downs says:

> Those of us who are most intolerant and judgemental of others' faults are inevitably even judgemental about ourselves. In private, we see ourselves as flawed and shameful. The expression of judgement upon others is nothing less than what we deliver to ourselves ... The more critical you are of others, the more difficult it is for you to reveal your true self to the world around you. When you have not allowed others to be less than perfect, does it not only follow that you can be less than perfect? And since you know you aren't perfect, how can you possibly reveal yourself? Creating an environment for authenticity requires that we give others the space to be authentic as well.[1]

For some, the path to being less judgemental will be to heal the shame that binds them.[2] That might involve the intervention of a good counsellor or therapist. When it has built up over a long period of time, shame can become deeply woven into our behavioural traits and characteristics. Much self-criticism comes from having internalized things others have said to us, often in childhood. It can take time and expertise to unpick and reframe that.

Directing our judgementalism inwards can also be an obstacle to our Christian faith. The theologian Daniel Migliore describes two ways sin corrupts our capacity to relate: the first where we think we can live without God; the second where low self-esteem causes us to see ourselves as less than we are. In both cases our hope of living fully human lives by relating properly to God and others is impeded.[3]

When we feel shame we worry unduly about what others think of us. This is a preoccupation of many teenagers, anxious to wear the right thing or act the right way in order to be accepted. The desire to be 'cool' can turn into a curse.

If we find we're still carrying those anxieties into later life then we're clearly not yet at ease with who we truly are. We become *pleasers*, always anxious to do the right thing to earn approval from those around us. But it doesn't matter how much validation is received, the same internal nagging voice is there to remind us that we are not good enough, and the real me, by whatever means, must never be seen.

But God sees us, and pours the light of acceptance and forgiveness onto us. 'GOD is sheer mercy and grace; not easily angered, he's rich in love. He doesn't endlessly nag and scold, nor hold grudges forever' (Psalm 103.8–9, *The Message*).

Francis Spufford writes about encountering God in stillness and silence, and the impact this divine encounter has on him: 'It knows the best of me, which may well be not what I am proud of, and the worst of me, which is not what it has occurred to me to be ashamed of.'[4] Spufford understands that there are limits to our self-knowledge (no matter how much we get tangled up in it), which God is able to see beyond and lead us through. The response is not condemnation. Jesus sympathizes with our weaknesses, having been 'in every respect . . . tested as we are, yet without sin. Let us therefore approach the throne of grace with boldness, so that we may receive mercy and find grace to help in time of need' (Hebrews 4.15–16).

If there is one institution where we should expect to have something to offer those who feel chronically shamed or self-critical, it is the Church, the bearer of Christ to the world. Alas, too much of the Church's history has instead seen it heaping shame on those it deems sinful or errant.

I don't believe Christians are any more judgemental than other people. I hope you will see from the above exploration of some root causes of judgementalism – tribalism, fear, blame, scapegoating, pride, ignorance, shame, low self-esteem – that this is a very human condition, rooted in our frailty and brokenness. But some Christians do seem to have used their faith as a platform from which to justify their judgementalism, and I firmly believe that their action is not rooted in the gospel but in the same fractured psychology that leads the rest of us to be intolerant of others and their behaviour.

We recently saw a Christian politician in Britain suggest that extreme weather conditions were God's judgement on the country for legislating in favour of gay marriage. When York Minster was devastated by fire there were those who proclaimed that it was God's judgement for, if I recall correctly, the then Bishop of Durham's 'heresy'. Many Christians still want to see, or imagine, God doling out damnation to those who do not agree with them.

It was so in Jesus' time too. His followers were deeply hopeful of a message of judgement full of hellfire and brimstone. Robert Farrar Capon writes:

> Indeed, so enamored were they of their own rockem-sockem, right-handed notions of divine crisis management that Jesus had a hard time getting through to them his essentially left-handed, noninterventionist view of the authentic judgment of God . . . The church, by and large, has always been more receptive to judgment-as-settling-scores than to judgment as proceeding out of, and in accordance with, the reconciling grace of resurrection.[5]

If nothing else, I hope this book will start a conversation about how our churches curb our urge to set others straight and reach out to them in love instead. In Part 2 we'll examine the teaching and example of Jesus to see what we learn from him about judgementalism. But I want to say two things to close Part 1 of this book.

The first is that by now you'll surely be wondering if I think we should never exercise judgement towards others. That's not what I think. Christ himself talks about 'right judgement' (John 7.24). However, having looked at the ways judgementalism can be self-serving to our ego, I hope you will see that executing such right judgement is tricky to master. Part 3 of this book will look at ways of nurturing our own spirituality in a way that disables the urge to judge, how we cultivate in its place discernment and empathy that is rooted in grace and how the Church walks the fine line between prophetic witness and egocentric judgementalism.

Second, there is a reason I think it's timely to consider this. I believe we live in an era where criticism and judgementalism have found a new impetus. A feature of these postmodern times is the rise of individualism. Scepticism towards authorities is increasing – whether Church, government/politics, science/medicine, justice or whatever. What matters to many is to avoid taking their cue from elsewhere and to follow instead their own instincts or whatever experience has taught them. People of my generation – Generation X, as I pointed out earlier – and younger feel a sense of entitlement to the best of life and want to feel we are important. All of which, it seems to me, points to a spiritual crisis that the Church could usefully speak into (but without wagging its finger). Thomas Moore writes:

> In many segments of culture today, having a lively intellectual life is considered 'nerdy.' It's 'cool' not to know anything about history and not to have a thought in your head. The meaning of life is often reduced to cruising with the popular culture. It doesn't take a course in psychoanalysis to glimpse severe anxiety behind this posture of know-nothingness. If

you had ideas and took yourself seriously, you would have to be constantly awake, educating yourself, and getting involved in your community. It's safer to hide out in a pretense of ignorance. For that is what 'cool' mindedness is, a way to sleep through life and not feel the sting and challenge of being engaged.[6]

Alongside all this, people have personal platforms through social media in which to broadcast their opinions and criticisms of others. And, after all, I am entitled to my opinion – although as one politician put it, 'Everyone is entitled to their own opinion, but not to their own facts.'[7]

You don't have to look far on social media to see how pernicious and ill-informed much of the content is, and positively hateful in places – not least towards public figures and celebrities these critics don't personally know but have read a very little about. Blogs and news websites now offer facilities for readers to comment on articles, and much of this is not edifying. This swirling miasma of judgementalism and intolerance is normalizing such behaviour, so that we feel entitled to wade in with our opinions or abuse.

There seems to be a growing intolerance towards other people's right to have an opinion, with the result that our capacity for nuanced debate is being diminished. In 2014, Scotland held a referendum to decide whether it should become an independent country. Opinions were passionately held and robustly expressed. One of the striking features of the debate leading up to the vote was how intolerant some people were of listening to opposing views – as if their right to an opinion overruled anyone else's right to a different one. It came to the point where some felt inhibited from revealing their voting intentions for fear of the anger and abuse they might receive. Twitter feeds and Facebook pages became filled with content to support one's views, personal propaganda tools that were more about telling others how to vote than exploring the arguments.

Whatever the field of public life, the common good cannot be well served if we lose the ability to debate issues rationally and respectfully without feeling we've somehow been personally violated when someone disagrees with us.

'Twitter spats', where public figures play out their disagreements to an audience of followers, have themselves become the subject of newspaper articles. And with only 140 characters in which to make your point, tweets are blunt, cutting and sometimes offensive. The Church is not immune to any of this. I've observed plenty of uncharitable Twitter arguments involving clergy and bishops, as well as assorted Christian bloggers – often hiding behind anonymity – who've established themselves as self-appointed authorities on whatever subject they care to write about.

As well as encouraging us all to express our opinions, the judgementalism present in digital media allows little room for redemption. People are accused, demeaned or dismissed before the writer swiftly moves on to talk about something else. The word 'trolling' has entered our vocabulary to describe someone who is deliberately inflammatory and offensive in their online remarks. Cyberbullying is becoming an issue of real concern as people hide behind the medium to say things they often wouldn't say to your face, or at least certainly not in the same terms.

Recently one female academic responded with such magnanimity and grace to being called a 'filthy old slut' by a student on Twitter that the story of her generosity became headline news. That it did so tells us something about how rare the qualities of forgiveness and kindness are in the online battle to fire ill-judged opinions and insults at each other.

Much of what happens online is simply an amplification of an age-old human predisposition to gossip about others. All social media does is offer a means to broadcast it to a much larger audience, often with little care for the consequences. Gossip's toxicity draws on the poison of judgementalism.

The Church's mission cannot be served by joining in with this cultural shift, and we need to broadcast a different message about how God stands apart from this: 'The voice of God is an affirming voice. It does not reduce us or belittle us. It seeks to enhance life. It speaks on behalf of life.'[8]

In this critical age, we should discover, through our behaviour and our message, how divine judgement stands apart from the intolerance humans direct at each other. Timothy Radcliffe writes:

> It is good news that the only judgement that matters is the last one, that of Christ. We are judged by others for our failures or our fatness, our laziness or ugliness, our stupidity or age. The media are always ready to judge everyone and find them guilty. We may even find ourselves before a judge in court and be found guilty of some crime. But thanks be to God, there is only one judgement that matters, the last one, and that is given by the merciful judge, who has already forgiven everything, if we will but accept his mercy.[9]

When we judge people rashly we dismiss and diminish them. Rather than bringing them into relationship with us we distance ourselves. Qualities of thoughtfulness and inquiry are set aside in favour of entrenching ourselves in our opinions. We cease to attempt to understand others and focus instead on defending ourselves and our views. We miss out on new opportunities and close down possibilities by making assumptions and jumping to conclusions. We buy into the myth that everything we need to know we've learned from our life experience, and in the process we reveal to others our lack of self-insight. We become pleased with ourselves and worship the power of our own intellect rather than being realistic about our limitations. We look down on others because of their failings, turning a blind eye to our own in the process. We set ourselves up as an authority over others without anyone granting it to us. We defend our ego and inner wounds by lashing out at others in the hope we'll draw attention from our own failings. Families crackle with tension; workplaces are undermined by mistrust; communities are poisoned by gossip; religious people assume they're better than others.

Surely there has to be a better way?

# *Part 2*

# JESUS AND JUDGEMENT

---

'Do not judge, so that you may not be judged.'
*Matthew 7.1*

# 7

## *How did Christians become so judgemental?*

---

> O wad some Pow'r the giftie gie us
> To see oursels as ithers see us!
> It wad frae mony a blunder free us,
> An' foolish notion:
> What airs in dress an' gait wad lea'e us,
> An' ev'n devotion!
> (Robert Burns, 'To a Louse, On Seeing
> One on a Lady's Bonnet at Church')

Humanity has long understood the perils of setting oneself above others – a theme frequently explored in art and literature – and yet we still struggle to acquire that most elusive of qualities, self-awareness. Robert Burns' oft-quoted verse above is best enjoyed noting the full title of the poem, which beautifully allows the whole scenario that inspired the piece to unfold in our imagination.

In the film *East is East* Ella, a white English mother, is seen braving the judgement and racism of her Salford neighbourhood as she strives to raise the family she has with her Pakistani husband. In response to one neighbour's self-righteousness, Ella's best friend sticks up for her, telling the woman to get lost before delivering the *coup de grâce*, 'And wash your bastard curtains, you dirty cow.'

I remember the burst of laughter this line provoked in the cinema audience. We love seeing people who get above themselves being taken down a peg or two. We recognize and disdain judgement that comes from those who've yet to put their own house in order. This is certainly a central element of soap operas, where cocky or arrogant characters get gradually more full of themselves while audiences eagerly await the moment they'll be put back in their box.

*East is East* is a drama with lots of themes – racism, gender, domestic violence. In particular it shows how the twin forces of tradition and religion wrongly applied can crush the flourishing of the human spirit.

That's an issue that vexed Jesus too, perhaps more than anything. He seems to have more to say about religious hypocrisy than almost anything else. While with one hand he reaches out in love to those in society who are stigmatized and castigated by others, he uses the other to point the finger at religious dogmatism that's lost any sense of compassion or love. It's a hollowed-out religion that plays the part of faithfulness to God while forgetting the very nature of God that we're called to adopt.

If it was a problem in Jesus' time it is no less so now, and Christians still fall into this trap. The American humourist David Sedaris captures this very well in a short story called 'If I Ruled the World':

> If I ruled the world the first thing I'd do is concede all power to the real King, who, in case you don't happen to know is Jesus Christ. A lot of people have managed to forget this lately, so the second thing I'd do is remind them of it. Not only would I bring back mandatory prayer in school, I'd also institute it at work. Then in skating rinks and airports. Wherever people live or do business, they shall know His name.

As the narrator hits his stride he begins to imagine Jesus helping him right all the wrongs he perceives around him.

> [Jesus] and I are going to work really well together. 'What's next on the agenda?' he'll ask, and I'll point him to the vegans and others who think their God is the real one. The same goes for the Buddhists and whoever it is that thinks cows and monkeys have special powers. Then we'll move onto the comedians with their 'F this' and 'GD that.' I'll crucify the

Democrats, the Communists, and a good ninety-seven percent of the college students. Don't laugh, Tim Cobblestone, because you're next! Think you can let your cat foul my flower beds and get away with it? Well think again![1]

Sedaris' story helps us to see the funny side of an unfortunate truth: sometimes the most judgemental people on earth are the followers of the one who said, 'Do not judge, so that you may not be judged' (Matthew 7.1). Timothy Radcliffe, in his book *What is the Point of Being a Christian*, says:

> A community which founded its existence on the claim to moral superiority would not only be repulsive but would inevitably invite people to search for our failures and expose them with glee. If the Churches are so often attacked in the press . . . then this is because it is generally but wrongly assumed that the point of being a Christian is to be better than other people.[2]

That 'general assumption' Radcliffe speaks of can, of course, be found in the Church just as much as outside it. It's hard to understand how anyone who seeks to put the gospel at the heart of their life could, even for a moment, think their mission is to be better than others.

Perhaps the Church has itself to blame for this. Too much emphasis on the 'I'm not worthy' and 'We are but miserable worms' school of theology could have misled us into thinking that salvation leads to a kind of superiority. It's true that we're saved by grace rather than anything we've done or deserve, but miserable wormology – so popular in the middle ages and beyond – probably didn't hurt the ruling classes' chance of keeping the lowly orders in their places. The theology may not be wrong but the emphasis certainly is these days, where levels of low self-esteem and anxiety are so poor.

And Christians are humans too. As we saw earlier, the drive for self-worth can easily lead to the sort of distorted behaviour where criticizing others diverts our energy from the more painful business of self-examination. One also wonders if those Christians similar to the character in David Sedaris' story above are taking their cue from society rather than Scripture.

The point of being a Christian isn't to be better than others – or even to engage in that sort of dualism. It's about how we relate to God and each other, working with the resources of discipleship – prayer, Scripture, Church and so on – to help us strengthen the quality of those relationships with a commodity called *love*.

That's a hard task. It's countercultural and contrary to human instinct. So God has given us Jesus Christ to show us how to live that way and, more importantly, to role-model it for us. Yes, really. We don't have to look far to understand what Christian living should look like, and that judgementalism has no place in it. Just open the New Testament at Matthew and start reading. You'll barely be on your second cup of coffee before you come to this:

> Don't judge people, and you won't be judged yourself. You'll be judged, you see, by the judgement you use to judge others! You'll be measured by the measuring-rod you use to measure others! Why do you stare at the speck of dust in your neighbour's eye, but ignore the plank in your own? How can you say to your neighbour, 'Here – let me get that speck of dust out of your eye,' when you've got the plank in your own? You're just play-acting! First take the plank out of your own eye, and then you'll see clearly enough to take the speck out of your neighbour's eye.                (Matthew 7.1–5)[3]

That translation is Tom Wright's, in his *Matthew For Everyone*. There he writes:

> Jesus warns against all such 'judgment'. He doesn't mean that we shouldn't have high standards of behaviour for ourselves and our world, but that the temptation to look down on each other for moral failures is itself a temptation to play God. And, since we aren't God, that means it's a temptation to play a part, to act, to be a 'hypocrite' (which literally means a play-actor, one who wears a mask as a disguise).[4]

We sometimes use the expression, 'I'll let God be the judge of that.' That truly should be our aspiration – instead of tilting our chins and pronouncing judgement on those around us (dirty curtains or no).

Previously we looked at how our judgement of others is unreliable because it's often an expression of our fears, anxieties and insecurities. In contrast to this, Jesus' judgement is pure. In John 5.30 he says, 'I can do nothing on my own. As I hear, I judge: and my judgement is just, because I seek to do not my own will but the will of him who sent me.' Only judgement properly tuned in to God is fair. As the Son of the Father, we can trust Christ's judgement in a way we can't our own and others' judgement. Our judgement is an expression of our own will rather than God's.

There's a tremendous freedom to be found in this. Once I recognize that my own judgement is always filtered through the distorted lens of my own psychological needs or experiences, it helps me to be much more suspicious of it. That's a great incentive to bite one's tongue. Instead we need to set our *self* aside and put God at the heart of the situation that troubles us.

That's another reason for being a Christian. The word 'sin' that the Bible uses to describe human behaviour can just as easily be rendered 'self-centredness'. It describes the human instinct to put ourself at the heart of life. At a basic level that might express itself as greed or selfishness. A more sophisticated aspect of sin is that our lives are so cluttered with our own baggage of experiences, opinions and sense of how things ought to be that we lose the ability to discern another person's behaviour without interpreting it from our own perspective. It's a short step from self-centredness to self-righteousness. So human judgement is always clouded.

This is why we've had to construct quite complex means of making legal judgments. A magistrate has to set his or her own opinion of the defendant and case aside and try to assess it in the light of the law instead. We know from countless miscarriages of justice over the years just how difficult a process that can be. And it's still worth a mention in the press when a judge, pronouncing judgement in a case, expresses concern that the law hasn't allowed handing down the sentence the defendant deserved.

Christian living is all about setting our self to one side and putting God at the heart of daily life. This is tough to do but when we persist in practising it we slowly become better. Barbara Mosse, commenting on John 5.30, says:

> In this life we can never be completely free from the influence of unconscious fears and motivations. But as we seek a closer relationship with God, our vision will be deepened and clarified, and we will increasingly be enabled to see the world through his eyes, rather than our own.[5]

You might say Christians are called to live their lives on the edge. The habit of stepping aside and putting Christ at the centre of all we do is one that takes a lifetime to cultivate. This is where I find the liturgy of confession at the start of our Eucharist helpful. As in many church traditions, our service begins by reflecting on the moments where we have put ourselves centre stage. Doing so helps me get back on track and redouble my efforts to place Christ there instead. Being a bit slow and stubborn, and with the accretion of over 50 years of unhelpful thought patterns and habits, I need – at least – a weekly reminder to drag me back on track.

The Catholic theologian James Alison calls this kind of living 'being on the periphery':

> This kind of being peripheral to a hugely benevolent powerful other is not the same as being 'marginal' at all. Since it includes the realisation that there is no one who is not just such a peripheral; and there is the possibility of being able to discover fellow peripherals, to whom I am able to relate as ones undergoing the same reception of inheritance and being called into rejoicing. But with a difference. None of us has to achieve anything, to get anything right, to be a success, and therefore it becomes possible to rejoice in others with whom I am in no sort of competition, and thus I do not need to protect myself against their mortality, their time-wasting, their deficiencies, or mine, because it is as such that we are liked and are being given to be something new.[6]

In other words, being peripheral is a great leveller. Whether we know it or not, choose it or not, God is central. As planets orbit the sun, held in place by its gravity, we exist in relation to a God who is the ground of our being. When we attempt to usurp God's place with our *self*, our ego or our fragile needs, we're only kidding ourselves. We're certainly not fooling God and much of the time we're not convincing anyone else either.

Once we understand that nobody else is central – no rich people, bosses, celebrities, politicians, monarchs, clergy, family members – we're freed from jostling for position. The path of our orbit is predetermined and we can't move from it. We can only pretend to. Or we could, as James Alison suggests, choose to relate to other people as co-peripherals we need not compete with or judge. We might then choose to reach out to them in love.

Some Christians lay great emphasis on God's judgement and see themselves and their Church as God's emissaries to put the world to rights. We'll look at questions about the Church's role in public morality and prophetic witness later on, but it's worth noting a curious thing at this point. Virtually none of the theological textbooks on my bookshelves list 'Judgement' in the contents page – not even a listing in the index. What you'll find listed is 'Reconciliation'. And here's the point: humanity's constant rejection of God doesn't lead to rejection in return. Instead God comes among us to restore us to himself. It's an action rooted in love, compassion and a longing for reconciliation. We learn that divine judgement is tempered by mercy and grace. God will do, and has done, whatever it takes to bring us back into relationship.

Even Jesus has little to say about it. Jim Wallis writes:

> There are very few passages of judgement in the New Testament, but [Matthew 25] is one of them. Jesus, unlike our religious institutions, constantly speaks out against judgementalism. But the only time Jesus is judgemental himself is on the subject of the poor.[7]

In the section of Matthew 25 to which Wallis refers (vv. 31–46), the Son of Man comes in glory to judge the nations, dividing the people in much the same manner a shepherd sorts sheep from goats in his flock. (That image makes little sense in the West, where our fat woolly sheep are easy to distinguish from their skinny cousins. In the Holy Land and elsewhere, sheep and goats are very similar.)

In the sheep–goat narrative Christ is saying that his judgement is very focused. It isn't about being straight or gay, married or cohabiting; it isn't about women who dare to contaminate the priesthood or episcopacy with their ministry or believe in their gender's right to choose; it isn't about how you celebrate the Eucharist/Holy Communion/Mass/Lord's Supper or even what you call it; it isn't about how many souls you've 'won for Christ' through your energetic evangelistic campaigns or how hard you pray or how long your prayer meetings last. In fact it isn't about any of the things the Church is often exercised about.

It's about caring for poor people.

Have we fed the hungry, welcomed the stranger, cared for the sick, visited those in prison? Well, have we? You wouldn't be alone in wondering why the Church isn't more vexed about these issues. Of course, Christians do undertake a great deal of work in these areas, much of it hidden. But given that Christ has said his judgement will be located in this arena, wouldn't we want to spend as much of our energy as possible on these causes; not let ourselves off the hook once we'd pushed a few charity envelopes through the neighbours' doors?

Jesus offers us fullness of life – life in which we flourish and grow closer to and become more like him. But religious judgementalism today so easily works against such life abundance, crushing the spirit and inhibiting the sometimes fragile work of inching towards wholeness – just as it did in Jesus' day. A common misunderstanding of divine judgement is that it operates as an extension of the same kind of judgements humans make of each other, intolerant of human failures and weakness. Jesus' teaching doesn't substantiate this view, his only express offering on the subject being that we won't be judged on our personal shortcomings – which are already forgiven – but called to account for our treatment of the poor. While human judgementalism is ultimately self-centred, obsessed with how well or badly others measure up to *our* expectations, Christ calls us out of ourselves and invites us to place God at the heart of our consciousness.

# 8

## The judge judged

The eminent twentieth-century theologian Karl Barth has helped much in our understanding of judgement. A section of his multi-volume *Church Dogmatics* is entitled 'The Judge Judged in Our Place'. Christ is our judge. Through his action on the cross he is also the one who bears the judgement that should rightfully be directed at us. The Church makes much of this in terms of atonement and in some traditions lays the message of personal salvation on thick. In doing so we risk missing a vital point.

The celestial courtroom drama that is presented has Christ in the dock as well as on the magistrate's bench. His divinity allows him to judge but it's his humanity that allows him to bear that judgement. While Christians are great at understanding how Jesus has managed to elbow us out of the dock, we're less good at seeing that he's also pushed us off the judgement seat – even while we still scrabble to get back on.

Barth writes, 'We are removed from the judge's seat, by the fact that Jesus Christ did for us what we wanted to do for ourselves.' How so? 'All sin has its being and origin in the fact that man wants to be his own judge.'[1]

It's our inability and unwillingness to leave judgement to God that puts us in conflict with God. We're setting ourselves up in opposition to God. This is really what's going on in the garden of Eden with Adam, Eve and the serpent. In consuming the forbidden fruit, Adam and Eve acquire the ability to tell good from evil. As the serpent puts it, 'you will be like God' (Genesis 3.5). Such is the power of human desire to judge ourselves and those around us. When we do that we play God – which stops God from being our God and prevents right relating between God and humanity.

'The fruit of this tree which was eaten with such relish is still rumbling in all of us', says Barth.[2]

Christ puts this right by taking over from us not only the role of the accused but also that of judge. In doing so we're liberated from the need to be judgemental (whether of ourselves in harsh self-criticism or others in self-justification), allowing us to put God back into that role and thus removing the obstacle that prevents proper relating. I've been – mostly – paying attention to sermons in church for the better part of 40 years, in different theological traditions, and I *never* heard anyone talk about that until I read Barth.

Some churches' theology emphasizes how we deserve to be judged, like errant children in need of a good spanking: it's only because Mr Jesus is so nice that he's kindly agreed to be spanked in our place, that we can be his friend once more (provided we're not naughty again – and if we are we must say sorry to him very quickly afterwards). This kind of Churchianity only tells part of the story and sets itself up as a nursery governess to regulate everyone's behaviour. If we constantly point the finger at our own – and other people's – naughtiness we completely lose sight of Christ's action in removing us from the judgement seat. And, in a massive irony, we forget in the process that it was the human desire to judge that got us into this mess in the first place.

It diminishes our understanding of sin – and infantilizes sinners – when we see it simply in terms of breaking God's rules. The interpretation of the events in Eden as naughty Adam and Eve not doing what they were told turns God into a rather vengeful deity who won't tolerate being crossed by humanity. The religions of Israel's neighbours were full of those kinds of gods. The understanding of the nature of God that's revealed in the Hebrew Scriptures, albeit one that emerges slowly over the long period in which they were written, is precisely that God is *not* the sort of petty, vindictive, untrustworthy, spat-prone monstrosity seen in the mythology of those poor sods who live over the border. This God, Yahweh, is loving and merciful, faithful, and keeps promises (covenant), is patient with wayward human behaviour but nonetheless acts out of grace to redeem them time and time again.

God isn't like humanity, nor like those gods based on human traits and behaviours. Yahweh is different and, in spite of our own bad behaviour, there's a part of us made in God's image that enables us to grow to be more godly and adopt those divine qualities.

The point of what happens in Eden is that humanity sets itself against Yahweh. By wanting the means to judge, humanity seeks to replace God. This is the obstacle, the barrier to right relating that the first sin creates. And God, in spite of our setting ourselves against God, refuses to become set against us. Because God is *for* us and not *against* us.

When you think about it, it's so much better having Christ as judge than one of our own. He's at once both kinder and harder than any human judge: kinder because he's someone who knows what it is to be human and has lived through the same experiences and situations as us – so his judgement is tempered with empathy; harder because his judgement brings into the light all we wouldn't care to admit to ourselves, all our self-deceptions and delusions. Barth writes that Christ's judgement is potentially something to be feared because of his power to pardon or condemn us. But it's not something we should be afraid of because Christ is a judge concerned with justice, with righting wrongs and upholding peace. His judgement 'indicates a favour, the existence of One who brings salvation'.[3]

Sometimes our judgements are rooted in a desire for power, control, revenge or punishment. We seek to exonerate ourselves while pronouncing others guilty. Christ's judgement operates within its own logic – that of grace. Divine judgement is so self-giving, says Barth, that 'it makes the enemies of God His friends'.[4] Christ comes to judge the world in such a way that grace is exhibited in the execution of judgement, to pronounce us free as judgement is passed. The logic of grace is beyond the scope of human reasoning. When we set ourselves up as judge of others it's not only impertinent but can often be so shockingly lacking in self-awareness that it's an embarrassment.

How does it feel to know our judgementalism has been rendered impotent by one who's not only prodded us off the magistrate's bench but then popped back up in the dock to take our place?

We might be tempted to feel threatened, peeved or thwarted. We might even feel annoyed that our need to justify ourselves by condemning others has been supremely torpedoed. Barth offers us another take on this. Why not try feeling liberated, he suggests, relieved of the burden of having to pass sentence on others all the time?

Through Christ's teaching and his role-modelling as someone fully human, we gain real insight into what it means to give up our judgementalism. Given that our capacity for judging others is corrupt and self-regarding, the person and ministry of Christ, as seen in the Gospels, offers us a different example against which we can measure ourselves – not as a means to keep punishing ourselves and others with criticism but to spur us on in self-giving Christian living.

# 9

## Breaking down barriers

—————•◦•—————

Having explored what it means for Christ to replace us as judge, we'd better remind ourselves of what it is to be redeemed. We've seen that our judgementalism can be directed at ourselves when we beat ourselves up over the things we feel inadequate or unworthy about. And judgementalism can also be a way of justifying ourselves by attacking others, which is how the damaged ego defends itself. Whether self-defence or self-criticism, judgementalism is seldom about the other person but rather an indicator of our own sense of value and self-worth.

The echoes of the Church's old miserable wormology ripple down to us today and do little to heal damaged egos or cultivate healthy humility. If a constant and unbalanced emphasis is placed on our unworthiness, how can Christ prise our white-knuckled fingers off the judge's bench? It's only when we accept that we're loved and redeemed through God's mercy and grace that healing can begin.

'We too often feel that God's love for us is conditional like our love is for others', says Desmond Tutu. 'We have made God in our image rather than seeing ourselves in God's image.'[1] God acts out of who God is, not out of who we are. In the Hebrew Bible, Daniel prays to Yahweh to have mercy on the people of Jerusalem at a time when they 'have become a disgrace' (Daniel 9.16). He seeks God's mercy not on the basis of his petition, nor any pretence about the righteousness of the people, but by reminding God that mercy is woven into the divine DNA. 'We do not present our supplication before you on the ground of our righteousness, but on the ground of your great mercies' (Daniel 9.18).

We can clearly see the healing power of merciful acceptance in the story of Jesus curing the slave of a Roman centurion (Luke 7.1–10). The centurion won't approach Jesus directly to ask for his slave to be made well but sends some Jewish elders with the message. Jesus sets off to the centurion's house, much to the Roman's alarm. He sends his friends out to meet Jesus with the message, 'I am not worthy to have you come under my roof; therefore I did not presume to come to you. But only speak the word, and let my servant be healed' (vv. 6–7).

The centurion assumes that, because he isn't a Jew, Jesus will take a dim view of him. Doubtless some of those watching these events unfold would have had clear prejudices about this pagan imperial occupier. But Jesus challenges any judgementalism there might be towards the outsider, as well as the centurion's own sense of worth.

As Paul Kennedy has written, two sorts of barriers are being broken down here. The centurion's *internal* self-criticism is challenged by Jesus' actions. In the same passage we see how well the Jewish elders speak of the centurion. He's a good Roman who loves the Jewish people, but the centurion seems unable to see beyond his own low self-worth. Christ restores him by praising him in front of the whole crowd. 'Not even in Israel have I found such faith' (v. 9), says Jesus, which was one in the eye for those who saw themselves as the object of divine favouritism. In saying this, Jesus also demolishes an *external* barrier: that of the social norm that divided Jew and Gentile, and the suspicion towards foreigners.

> The Christian call to holiness is associated with wholeness and an integrated personality. This is achieved when we accept and embrace the damaged parts of our ego, seeing ourselves as Christ sees us. To both us and Christ, our own damaged nature is visible, and still he wants to come under our roof.[2]

This sense of being accepted by Christ plays a vital part in healing our judgementalism. We know we aren't perfect, but to fixate on our perceived inadequacies is to erect a barrier to Christ's redemptive action. We must own for ourselves the words of St Paul when he says, 'There is . . . now no condemnation for those who are in

Christ Jesus' (Romans 8.1). I rather like the way Eugene Peterson renders this in *The Message*: 'Those who enter into Christ's being-here-for-us no longer have to live under a continuous, low-lying black cloud . . . Christ, like a strong wind, has magnificently cleared the air.'[3]

When we accept that we're free to breathe in that clean fresh air, not because we've earned it or done anything to deserve it but because it's given simply out of the nature of who God is, then we can start to shake off the impetus to judge self and others.

Writing in a newspaper editorial about debates on whether people deserve welfare, Catherine Pepinster says:

> Christianity stands firm in its diametric opposition to the cold calculation of who deserves what. There is no moment in the parable of the Good Samaritan for cautious assessment of the hapless mugged victim lying by the side of the road. It matters neither who he is nor what side of any divide he might belong. His humanity is enough.[4]

(It is, of course, those who walk by on the other side who come off worst in this parable.) How different Pepinster's article is from much newspaper comment, littered with judgement on who has it coming to them – or at least deserves to – or is to blame for [insert topical issue of your choice here]. Pepinster speaks Christian truth into a media culture of blame and judgement that we Christians all too easily buy into.

In addition, the Church sometimes acts as gatekeeper to God's mercy, insisting on clear, sometimes public, acts of repentance before pronouncing God's forgiveness. Confession is, of course, helpful in nurturing our own spiritual growth. There's a big difference between the Church facilitating private and corporate repentance for our personal and common good, and an imposed test of who should be welcome and who rejected – not least because those who establish 'in'-ness and 'out'-ness have already accepted Christ's assurance that they're 'in' yet seem troubled by the possibility that others who aren't at all like them might also be declared in by the cross. That's little different from the religious and popular mindset that Jesus encountered and challenged in his day.

In fact Jesus tackles this tendency to determine who's in and who's out in his parable about a wheat field riddled with weeds (Matthew 13.24–30, 36–43). When the landowner's servants see that there are weeds growing among his crop of wheat, they itch to pull them out. The landowner prevents them, fearing that in pulling up the weeds they'll also remove some of the wheat and damage the yield. Better, he says, to leave it until harvest. Cut everything at the same time, then separate the wheat and send the weeds off to be burnt.

This is a parable about judgement. Leave it to the Son of Man to sort out the causes of evil, says Jesus. If you're busy squabbling about who should be in the wheat field and who shouldn't, you're simply going to damage the harvest. The work of the Church in building for God's kingdom is diminished when our energy goes into deciding who we find acceptable and who not. We don't have to look far to see how the Church's reputation has been damaged by such squabbling, or the numbers who've stopped attending because they can't bear the self-regarding hypocrisy they encounter. Leave it to God.

Here we understand what it might mean to trust in God – not the glib 'Will he save me a parking space?' kind of trust that centres on self or our daily preoccupations, but a trust that the story of humanity and creation is in God's hands, a trust that believes the work of the kingdom is a long game that arches beyond the time span in which we tend to demand satisfaction (that is, soon if not now). In fact much of Scripture is about recording the work of God over long periods of time: think of the children of Israel in slavery in Egypt for centuries, their long years as desert wanderers or in captivity in Babylon. People would have been born, grown up and died within these time spans. These stories serve to remind us that God is still at work, even when our patience runs out.

I remember taking the funeral of a woman who had died after a long stay in hospital. She was a devoted reader of fiction and passed away when she was just a couple of chapters from the end of an 800-page novel. I wasn't only touched by this footnote to the woman's life but surprisingly upset that she never learned how the plot resolved. How unjust, I thought. Yet I can see that this is what a life of faith involves. To trust God means relinquishing any expectation that I might get to see how the story ends in my lifetime – or see God's promised reign of justice and peace come to pass in the situations that bother me today. Which monstrous dictators will be overthrown? When will peace break out in the Middle East? How will wealth come to be more fairly distributed so that no one need be hungry or homeless?

Leaving judgement to God requires me to pull back from the immediate and see the bigger picture, the long game of God. In spite of knowing this, I still find it hard to give up the habit of judgement – not least when it's going on all around me. And society is often at its worst when it collectively scapegoats a whole category of people, as we'll see next.

# 10

## *The offer of loving acceptance*

---

Society has a habit of excising certain kinds of people from public acceptability. They become toxic in the collective consciousness. Bankers and city traders suffered a bit of this following the credit crunch of 2008 and resulting recession. They were tarred with the same brush in the minds of many – without much discernment for the great variety of banking sectors and jobs within them.

Abusers of children are reviled to such an extent that it's perfectly acceptable to wish them ill, to a degree that would be shocking if we were talking about anyone else.

Some of what's going on here is the kind of scapegoating we looked at earlier: I make myself feel better – self-righteous – when I condemn the perpetrators of actions much worse than anything I've done. It's more challenging to swallow the hard truth that God loves them just as much as he loves me: 'the Lord is the judge, and with him there is no partiality' (Ecclesiasticus 35.15).

In first-century Palestine, tax collectors were among the greatest social pariahs of the day. They were presumed to be corrupt, making themselves wealthy by cheating hard-pressed taxpayers. They were perhaps also seen as collaborators with the occupying Romans, rendering them especially loathsome. So, naturally enough, Jesus makes a beeline for them. Not only does he call a tax collector to be one of the 12 disciples (Matthew), but in Luke 19 we read about his encounter with another (Zacchaeus).

Jesus is visiting the city of Jericho and is surrounded by a great crowd. Trying to get a look-in is Zacchaeus, who is: (i) not just a tax collector (boo!) but a top-ranking tax collector (extra boo!); (ii) filthy rich, having swindled taxpayers for personal profit; (iii) short in physical stature. He wants sight of Jesus too but isn't tall enough to see over the heads of others – and given what he does for a living, the crowd doesn't feel greatly disposed to let him through. So he climbs a tree for a better view, which is where Jesus finds him.

At this point, where sinner encounters Saviour, many Christians would expect the following to happen:

1 person is confronted with his wickedness and called to repent;
2 sinner repents of his evil ways;
3 Jesus forgives him;
4 sinner becomes a Christian and enters into relationship with Christ and the fellowship of believers.

Plenty of evangelism today operates on this model, which does rather lend itself to the gatekeeping role some churches take on for themselves. If your approach to outreach requires the rigid sequential approach above, it's easy to fall into the trap of demanding that stage 2 has been satisfactorily accomplished (and perhaps even publicly demonstrated) before moving on to stages 3 and certainly 4, where we will only agree to admit you to the fellowship of believers once we're properly satisfied you've actually repented and really, truly mean it – and preferably have transformed into an upright, Bible-carrying character of good standing. In this scenario, conversion is a moment in time and Christians take on for themselves the role of judge in scrutinizing how genuine a convert is.

That isn't what happens to Zacchaeus.

Zacchaeus is transformed through an encounter with loving acceptance rather than judgement. There are no preconditions to Jesus' entering Zacchaeus' house. All the tax collector has to do is open his door to Christ, a decision made much easier knowing Jesus isn't looking down on him (figuratively speaking at least . . .). Jesus simply wants to be his friend. This is a very radical kind of conversion. Zacchaeus is changed by an encounter in which he's made to feel good about himself by Jesus, in a context in which nobody else will do that for him.

Indeed there is a chorus of grumbling among those who witness the scene. 'He has gone to be the guest of one who is a sinner', they complain (Luke 19.7). They're playing the in-or-out game, wanting to weed out someone who fails to live up to their own self-righteousness. What a shock, then, that Jesus chooses Zacchaeus over them. This is what Christ does again and again in the Gospels: he strolls past the folk who believe they're part of God's in-crowd and reaches out to the untouchables, the scandalous, the swindlers and the hookers. Jesus Christ! You mean the kingdom of God is for the likes of *them*?

Zacchaeus, meanwhile, is discovering what it means to be one of the dregs made holy. He volunteers to give away half of his property to poor people and to repay anyone he's swindled with four times whatever he cheated them out of. He changes his behaviour as a consequence of his encounter with God's love. Change isn't a condition imposed on Zacchaeus before he's welcomed in. It's the welcome itself – and a powerful encounter with loving acceptance (stage 3) – that converts him.

How would the Church look if this warts-and-all welcome were freely offered, rather than a pressure to conform? Some churches do accomplish this, but sadly there's no shortage of others where the welcome – and I mean a deep welcome to participate fully in the life of the Church – is conditional.

When I'm in central London and have a few minutes to spare, I like to go and sit in the church of St Martin-in-the-Fields on Trafalgar Square. It's refreshing to step inside, away from the roar and crush of traffic and crowds, and sit for a few moments of rest and contemplation. But it's seldom completely quiet. More often than not, deep snoring is heard from the back pews, quite often in a range of keys and accents. Sheltered from the elements, the homeless of the West End come here to stretch out and catch up on a bit of kip.

The snores of St Martin's are an expression of hospitality, a mustard seed of the kingdom of God out of which can grow a beautiful tree that offers rest, welcome and shade. Such gestures, not without their headaches or complaints I'm sure, are a gentle step in practising the sort of loving non-judgement Jesus shows to Zacchaeus, the centurion and others.

There is, however, something transformational in their experience as the objects of Christ's love. Rather than seeing repentance – a word that means to 'turn around' – as a prerequisite mechanical action that jerks God's chain and dishes out a dose of forgiveness, we see in these stories that mercy and grace are already present to us and that being exposed to them brings about the turning around. This is what the Church has to offer as the bearer of Christ to the world today – if only we can stop our judgementalism getting in the way.

Jesus constantly surprises his followers by touching the frowned upon and drawing them into his circle of friends. As Brian McLaren puts it:

> Jesus' secret message in word and deed makes clear that the kingdom of God will be radically, scandalously inclusive . . . It takes a while for his followers to realize where this will lead, but they eventually get it: they realize that in the kingdom of God, they can no longer label people with old labels like male/female, Jew/Gentile, slave/free, rich/poor, Barbarian/ Scythian, and so on. They must see people in a new light. When they see people as God's creations, beloved by the King and welcome in the kingdom, they must open their hearts, homes, tables, and fellowships to everyone, without regard for old distinctions.[1]

The snap judgement and assessments we make of other people, the prejudices we bear against people not like us, have no place in the kingdom of God that Christ proclaims.

In our own time, who do we resist welcoming into the fellowship of God's kingdom? To whom do we put up barriers, expecting their values, culture, behaviour or identity to change before we allow them to be baptized, receive communion, get confirmed or hold office? Might it even be the case that our own lack of loving acceptance is the impediment that prevents folk from encountering the transformational turnaround-inducing love of Jesus?

# 11

## *Seeing ourselves, and others, for who we really are*

—————•◦•◦•—————

If Jesus shocked self-righteous onlookers by reaching out to tax collectors and Romans, there are other occasions when he manages to tread on several taboos at once. John, in his Gospel, suggests there are no witnesses to Christ's scandalous breach of etiquette in striking up a conversation with a Samaritan woman. Probably just as well – that's a shocking double whammy right there: a Samaritan *and* a woman.

There was plenty in Jewish religious practice and social custom to warn Jesus to avoid any interaction with the woman he finds drawing water from the well. True to form, then, he heads straight for her (strike 1), starts a conversation (strike 2) and asks to drink from her water pot (strike 3). If the priests and scribes had witnessed any of this there would've been a major run on defibrillators.

The people of Samaria were the product of several particular historical twists and turns. Following the death of King Solomon, the kingdom of Israel split in two, with Judah in the south – centred on the capital, Jerusalem – and Israel in the north. The city of Samaria was built as the new capital of the northern kingdom, its name eventually coming to apply to the whole region. Later the northern kingdom was conquered by Syrians. They settled there and the population began to interbreed. Meanwhile their faith, still centred on the five books of Moses, evolved into something rather different from the Judaism of the southern kingdom. By the time of Christ, Samaritans were viewed by Jews as both foreign and heretical.

Isn't it sometimes the case that our strongest judgements are reserved not for those most different but those quite similar to us? Do we feel more threatened by those with whom we share much in common but see as having deviated from our own values or social norms? Think of Catholics and Protestants in Ireland (or my part of Scotland even); centre-left liberals and centre-right conservatives in politics; gay and straight – well, everywhere. And in many cultures the offspring of parents from two different religions attract particular prejudice – even though they're half the same as those who reject them.

They may have loathed each other but by the time of Christ, Judeans and Samaritans were living side by side under Roman occupation. If you wanted to travel from Jerusalem to Galilee – as Jesus is doing at the start of John 4 – you had to pass through Samaria. Any interaction with Samaritans would be kept to an absolute minimum, and Jewish men didn't as a rule engage with women. Once again Jesus plays with people's judgements about outsiders.

Like Zacchaeus, the woman at the well's personal morality is open to question, yet the dialogue with Jesus doesn't begin with his judging or calling her to repentance. Instead she's freely offered the water of life – an internal transformation leading to full and abundant living. Indeed even when Jesus raises the question of her many husbands and her current out-of-wedlock relationship, it's less a judgement and more of an insight offered to demonstrate his messiahship.

Cynthia Bourgeault sees in this episode a fascinating heart-to-heart:

> He sees who she is; she sees who he is. And in the light of that mutual recognition they keep on empowering each other and drawing each other along to greater self-disclosure, until finally, a few lines later, Jesus says to her, 'The hour is coming and is even now here when the true worshipers will worship the Father in spirit and in truth, for that is the kind of worship the Father wants.' The woman replies, 'I know that the Messiah, that is the Christ, is coming. When

he comes he will tell us everything.' Jesus said, 'I, who am talking to you, I am he.'

What an extraordinary moment! It is the first time in this
gospel that Jesus reveals his true identity to anyone.[1]

That disclosure is all the more powerful because the hearer is
someone very firmly judged 'out' by the temple elite. It isn't the
Pharisees, priests or scribes who get to understand who Jesus is,
rather he chooses to reveal himself to someone beyond the pale
as far as they're concerned. What I love about this exchange is
that, like Jesus' parables, truth and understanding are only revealed
by wrestling with and questioning what Jesus is saying – a task to
which this woman is more than equal. 'Far from being intimidated,'
Bourgeault writes, 'she returns his serve beautifully.'[2] Challenging
him, upping the ante, the intenseness and boldness of the exchange
bring insight and transformation for the woman.

This is somebody really showing us what it means to have a
relationship with Christ; not a neatly tied up set of religious dogma
or formularies we mentally adopt but a living dialogue rooted in
prayer, imagination and spirit. For the woman that journey starts
not with judgement but with grace. Rather than condemning her
for her marital life, Jesus simply reaches out to her in love, draws
her in and brings her into relationship with him. Is this how Christ's
Church today reaches out to those whose lifestyle it judges immoral?
If this woman wandered into your congregation and told her story,
would she be lovingly received and drawn into fellowship, or told
where she had to put her life in order first?

Christ is our judge but in his earthly ministry, time and again,
he shows us by his example how to set our judgementalism aside.
He touches those judged most harshly by society with his grace
rather than his condemnation. Secure in who he is, Christ has no
need to make himself feel bigger by heaping scorn on others.

One of the most dramatic examples of this occurs in John 8,
where a woman is presented to Jesus having been accused of
adultery. It's worth reading that passage in full:

Early in the morning he came again to the temple. All the
people came to him and he sat down and began to teach

them. The scribes and the Pharisees brought a woman who had been caught in adultery; and making her stand before all of them, they said to him, 'Teacher, this woman was caught in the very act of committing adultery. Now in the law Moses commanded us to stone such women. Now what do you say?' They said this to test him, so that they might have some charge to bring against him. Jesus bent down and wrote with his finger on the ground. When they kept on questioning him, he straightened up and said to them, 'Let anyone among you who is without sin be the first to throw a stone at her.' And once again he bent down and wrote on the ground. When they heard it, they went away, one by one, beginning with the elders; and Jesus was left alone with the woman standing before him. Jesus straightened up and said to her, 'Woman, where are they? Has no one condemned you?' She said, 'No one, sir.' And Jesus said, 'Neither do I condemn you. Go your way, and from now on do not sin again.'

(John 8.2–11)

For all that adultery was against the law of Moses, Jesus sees here a greater wrong: a 'deep-rooted sin which uses the God-given law as a means of making oneself out to be righteous, when in fact it is meant to shine the light of God's judgment into the dark places of the heart'.[3]

My relationship with judgement should be that it is for me and not for other people. I ought to hold on to Christ's instruction to 'first take the log out of your own eye, and then you will see clearly to take the speck out of your neighbour's eye' (Matthew 7.5). This isn't so I can beat myself up about my shortcomings but rather allow my relationship with God through Christ to help me discern the right path for godly living, modelled on the example of Jesus. This relocates judgement from simply being a one-off 'end of times' event and brings it into the here and now. Christ's role-modelling offers a benchmark that spurs me on towards greater wholeness (that is, holiness). Judgement in this sense becomes motivational rather than condemnatory, but it's a tricky balancing act.

I have to remember that I fall short of the standards God has set for me and, to be fair, the standards I expect of myself. Confession – whether personal or corporate – is the place where I bring my mistakes into the open before God. They won't be news to God, who's already got a pretty good handle on human shortcomings. Nonetheless God's loving forgiveness allows me to let go of them so that I'm unburdened of the despondency created by continually letting myself down. Spending time in this prayerful place helps me focus on how I *might* be instead. Divine judgement in this sense is a process of self-examination conducted in the presence of God and in the knowledge of what Christ has done for us. This is judgement as illumination, opening up the darkest recesses of my heart and mind to the light of the world so that I can better see what's lurking in there: 'he takes my side and executes judgement for me. He will bring me out to the light' (Micah 7.9).

Having been relieved of the burden of my wrongdoing I mustn't make the mistake of comparing myself to others – neither those I imagine holier than me, risking poor self-esteem, nor those I consider worse offenders than me, fuelling self-righteousness. 'Let anyone among you who is without sin be the first to throw a stone at her' (John 8.7). Jesus reminds the scribes and Pharisees that they're in no position to judge and that their self-righteousness is even more problematic to holy living than the woman's adulterous behaviour.

Fast-forward 2,000 years and the Church is still getting its knickers in a twist about other people's sexual behaviour, seemingly more so than it does about inequality, the needs of the poor, the misuse of power and the reeking hypocrisy of the self-righteous. Why might this be? Is there something about our own unexpressed sexual desires that makes us uncomfortable? Is the only way we can imagine purging that discomfort by scapegoating others whose sexuality is more visible?

Perhaps what Jesus is asking the crowd – mindful that he's also taught that even looking at others in lust is as bad as stripping off and getting down to it with them – is: 'Which one of you has never fancied another person's partner, imagined what it might be like with someone of the same sex or with a whole group of people, clicked that link in a spam email that you know will take you nowhere good, wanted to dress up in a uniform, be restrained, get out the flying helmet and the wet celery or whatever else floats your boat? Let whoever's mind has never wandered off in any of those directions come forward and throw the first stone at this woman.'

He's not saying her adultery doesn't matter, but he refuses to condemn her and urges her to go and sin no more. In his splendid and provocative polemic in defence of Christian faith, Francis Spufford writes:

> [Jesus] seems weirdly unbothered about sex. Except to make it clear that it falls under the umbrella of his perfectionism, he hardly has a thing to say about it . . . He does not denounce anything. He does not seem to be disgusted by anybody, anybody at all. It is as if, shockingly, what we do in bed is not specially important to him . . . On the other hand, he has a *lot* to say about self-righteousness.'[4]

This isn't the same as saying anything goes, and the Church has an important role in helping us relate meaningfully to one other and, by extension, consider how our sexuality can deepen and enrich relationships in a way that gives us a glimpse of the divine. But surely we've passed the point where we need exert so much energy getting vexed about anything that deviates from the missionary position. To be frank, people banging on about others' sex lives makes me wonder what's going on in *their* fantasy lives that alarms them so much.

Remember the American evangelist who denounced homosexuality at every opportunity, then was discovered in a motel room with a rent boy? That's it.

Thomas Moore, a former monk and now psychotherapist, sees in the Church's discomfort with matters sexual an unwillingness or inability to acknowledge that we all have what Carl Jung called a shadow side.

> However you present yourself to the world, on some level you are a dark person. You have thoughts you don't usually

tell people. You are capable of things that your friends may know nothing about. You are probably more interesting sexually than the world realizes. You probably have some anger and fears that you don't tell people about. You may have secrets from your past that make you more intriguing than your persona would suggest. Certainly your potential for darker thoughts and behavior is rich.[5]

Christ embraces all of this, even though we may not do so within ourselves. His conversations with the women above take the shadow side as read. He doesn't feel the need to make a song and dance about it the way we might or the religious leaders of his day certainly did. He has no need to scapegoat others to make himself feel better about his own shadow side. He simply offers to illuminate our inner life so that we can come to terms with our darkness and learn that we're loved in our entirety. When we face up to our own darkness and acknowledge it, when we recognize that it doesn't make God love us any the less, we can come to a better understanding of who we really are. And by dropping the pretences that come when we attempt to cut ourselves off from our own darkness, we stand a better chance of being less judgemental about the manifestations of darkness we see in those around us.

# 12

## *Tearing the doors off their hinges*

———•◦•———

There are times when it seems that in his storytelling Jesus deliberately toys with our enthusiasm for making judgements about others, then having lured us in he delivers a magnificent twist at the end. The parable of the prodigal son is a good example of this.

The younger of two sons yearns for his freedom and independence. He can't afford to leave home but hasn't got the patience to wait to inherit his share of the estate. With immense impertinence he asks his father for his share now. Astonishingly the father agrees, and the son departs for a life of reckless living and partying. Inevitably, it isn't long before he's blown all the cash and become destitute. Heading home with his tail between his legs, he hopes his father might give him a labouring job on the estate.

'A clip round the ear'ole, more like. Really! You treat your father like he means nothing, go your own sweet way and when it all goes pear-shaped, have the cheek to swan back in here and expect to be bailed out. You've got a nerve.' That's his mother talking, by the way. In my mind she sounds a lot like Barbara Windsor in full-throttle, behind the bar of The Queen Vic. The mother doesn't appear in the story Jesus tells, but if she did I bet that's just what she'd say. And quite right too. He had it coming.

How does the story leave you feeling about the son at this point? If you're a parent, what's your reaction to this boy's behaviour? How would you respond to being treated so expendably? Jesus has set the bait on the hook and starts to reel us in with our judgementalism in full flow. 'Teach him a lesson', we might say; 'Make him pay you back'; 'Don't let him walk all over you.'

Three months after I passed my driving test, at the age of 18, I drove my parents' brand new Volvo into the rear of an unsuspecting Peugeot. I'd come flying over the brow of a hill, late for an appointment, and wasn't expecting to find a stationary car waiting to turn right. There were no injuries, thankfully, and I was able to drive the car home. Visibly shaking, and with the car's right wing and bonnet crumpled, my mother was at the door before I made it up the garden path. Expecting the massed ranks of all the furies of hell to be unleashed, my father had only one thing to say to me: 'Are you hurt, son?'

It was over 30 years ago, but it moves me to tears to recall it. This was a prodigal son experience, where all the judgement and punishment one could rightfully imagine is set aside in favour of love. 'But while he was still far off, his father saw him and was filled with compassion: he ran and put his arms around him and kissed him' (Luke 15.20).

One can imagine Jesus' listeners rapt with attention at this point – 'We weren't expecting that.' But there's yet more to this story. The father's celebration in welcoming his son home puts the elder brother's nose out of joint. He's the one who brings judgementalism and self-righteousness into this story ('You've never thrown a party like this for me, and I've been a much better son than him – hardworking, obedient, loyal. And *him* – after all he's done to you.')

> The parable's concluding image – of the older son standing alone outside, refusing to join the party because he feels he has been slighted – is a vivid symbol of the way the egoic operating system holds us back from joining the dance of Divine Mercy in full swing all around us. If we're stuck in the ego, we can't hear the music.[1]

Judgementalism rooted in self-righteousness blinds us to the wideness of God's mercy. Making comparisons between ourselves and others can easily leave us isolated, wallowing in self-pity or clinging on in splendid arrogance. When we rejoice at God's grace being extended to those around us we can more fully participate in the kingdom. In church life the petty judgements we make of one another, the schisms and splinters, the 'Who-does-she-think-she-is?'s all serve to draw us away from entering into the realm of love and life God offers us.

Perhaps my favourite of Jesus' parables is the story he tells of a vineyard owner hiring some workers to bring in his harvest (Matthew 20.1–16). The grape-picking takes longer than expected, so every two or three hours he goes to the marketplace to hire more workers. When all is gathered in the workers are each paid exactly the same amount, regardless of how long they worked. When those who've been working the longest realize that others have put in far fewer hours for the same wage, resentment boils over.

The parable points to the extravagance and impartiality of God's mercy. There are people to whom God opens his arms who've done far worse things than you, lived more recklessly, caused a good deal more harm to those around them. It might be galling – but only for those too wrapped up in their own self-importance. The humble will recognize that it can be no other way.

Francis Spufford suggests that one of 'Christianity's most destructive failures [is] our persistent desire to give grace a down-grade'.[2] Writing about this parable he says:

> Jesus offered the very gentle, easy-way-in story of labourers who all get paid the same no matter when they turn up for work, but there are far harder, far more revolting con-sequences to grace. It is not for us to know who does and does not manage to accept forgiveness, but if the love really never stops, if God really does long for every lost soul, then in principle God regards as forgivable a whole load of stuff we really don't want forgiven, thank you. People who use airliners to murder thousands of office workers, people who strut about Norwegian summer camps stealing the lives of teenagers with careful shots to the head, people who drive over their gay neighbour in their pick-up truck and then reverse and do it again, people who torture children for sexual pleasure: God is apparently ready to rush right in there and give them all a hug, the bastard. We don't want that. We

want justice, dammit, if not in this world then in the next. We want God's extra-niceness confined to deserving cases such as, for example, us, and a reliable process of judgement put in place which will ensure that the child-murderers are ripped apart with red-hot tongs.[3]

The desire for vengeance that sometimes fuels our judgementalism seeks to redirect attention from our own shortcomings and point out, 'Look! There's someone over there much worse than me.' It's like the magician who tries to pull off a trick by misdirecting the audience's attention.

Quite a number of Jesus' parables are about judgement – some of those we haven't looked at include the parables of the coins, the wicked tenants, the wise and foolish virgins, the talents or the faithful and unfaithful servants – and they always have a capacity to surprise us. They've also done much to form the bedrock of the Church's errant judgementalism. These are stories that need handling with care, and sometimes we should be far less po-faced in our reading of them. We don't always get to see when Jesus has his tongue in his cheek, or to whom in his audience he was particularly directing his message.

A common thread that runs through them is that we are in-cluded in the kingdom of God unless we choose to exclude our-selves. One parable where we see this set out – and also has Jesus at his most hyperbolic – is the story of the wedding banquet in Matthew 22.1–14.

A king has arranged a wedding banquet for his son. When the time comes he sends out his servants to fetch the guests, but none of them will attend. When the servants report back to the king he sends them out a second time with the message, 'I've gone to all this trouble and it's going to be a really terrific party – you won't be sorry you came.' But the invited guests make light of it, some going off to work while others abuse and murder the servants.

The king is enraged by this and sends in the troops. Like the denouement in a James Bond movie, commandos dropping from a height, slithering down ropes, guns blazing and lobbing grenades until all the invited guests are killed and their homes destroyed.

The king then sends his servants out into main streets to bring in *everyone*, 'both good and bad' (v. 10), until the banquet hall is absolutely full. 'Right,' says the king, 'Let's party!' And they do. They kick off their sandals and absolutely whoop it up, their differences set aside as they get on with the main job of joining in with the king's happiness at the marriage of his son.

It's all going great guns until the kings spots, lurking in a corner, one man. He's not made any effort to smarten himself up and isn't joining in with the feasting or the dancing – just stands their scowling, arms folded. The king can't believe it. 'What's not to like about this?' He's not going to have a sourpuss spoiling the party so gets a bouncer to throw him out.

I've never met our Queen. I know that if there's a royal wedding I won't find my name on the guest list. Westminster Abbey will be full of the great and the good: dignitaries, other monarchs, presidents and politicians, establishment figures, courtiers, maybe even the odd celebrity. In short, all the people against whom a monarch would normally rub. They're the royal equivalent of the in-crowd. Can you imagine none of them turning up, and the Queen sending in the troops to sort them out?

Much in this parable is heightened and exaggerated to make a point. The party is the kingdom of heaven; the king is God; the in-crowd who've been invited but don't show up are the temple elite – all who think they're a shoo-in for God's favouritism. It turns out, though, that they haven't really responded to God's invitation at all, for all their posturing and show-offiness, their self-righteousness and their casual disregard for those they look down on. So God throws open the gates and ushers everyone in – everyone, good and bad. The only fly in the ointment is Mr Slouchy in the corner. What does he do wrong to get himself evicted? He doesn't join in (just like the elder brother of the prodigal son). That's all there is to it. God's open welcome and invitation into his kingdom is for all. You don't earn your way in. You don't have to be a pope or a bishop. You don't have to have a clean record with no points on your licence. You don't need never to have been caught doing something naughty. Your face doesn't have to fit or your table manners be finishing-school standard. You don't need never to have made a bad decision in your life, or a whole string of bad decisions. You don't need to conform the way your local church wants you to. You just have to not say 'no'. Robert Farrar Capon writes:

> The only thing that can possibly be a problem for the kingdom is a faithless nonacceptance of God's having solved the problem of evil all by himself, and without ever once having mentioned the subject of reform. He does not invite the good and snub the bad. He invites us all, while we are yet sinners.[4]

What Jesus points to, again and again, is the appalling truth that the people we think don't deserve God's grace are covered by it to exactly the same degree as we are. And while somehow shocking, this is ultimately so liberating, so freeing. There's no need to keep up with the Jones's, no need to seek the vicar's favour, beat ourselves up if we've made more mistakes than the next person. We're no less welcome because we need a drink or two to get through the day, have been divorced three times or really do fantasize about things too rude for polite conversation – all those things Christians sometimes look down on in others in pity, only to be faced with Jesus' shocking retort: 'You're no better than them – but you're no worse either, so come on in.'

And like Zacchaeus, we can all be transformed when we encounter the radical hospitality and inclusiveness of that grace. The challenge for churches is how to offer that. Too often we feel the urge to tell people what's wrong with their lives, that they need to put their house in order before they can join our exclusive club – demanding transformation first and offering grace second, as if it's ours to dispense. We set ourselves up as gatekeepers to the kingdom, while Jesus has asked us to do no such thing, pointedly ripping the gates off their hinges to stop his followers appointing themselves as divine bouncers.

There are no terms and conditions to accepting the king's invitation, no courses you need to go on, no rituals you have to undertake, nobody you have to please before you're welcomed in. You just have not to say 'no' to the invitation.

While Jesus' parables may sometimes play with our judgemen-talism, he warns us not to listen to them with narrow-minded judgement. After telling the parable of the sower he says, 'Pay atten-tion to what you hear; the measure you give will be the measure you get, and still more will be given you' (Mark 4.24). In other words, you'll be judged to the degree of your own judgementalism. Robert Farrar Capon again:

> If you have any feeling for the way narrow minds work, you will realize that the Sower, as told, would immediately strike such minds as reeking of the catholicity they had spent their entire religious lives deploring. People who are that narrow do not really listen to what someone says; rather, they sniff at his words – they check them over to spot the squishy, rotten spots through which ideas they hate might seep in.[5]

Christ also knows that he's on the receiving end of people's judge-ment, not least because his own message about God's merciful judgement sits so badly with what humans expect. First-century Jews wanted divine judgement that would come down, duff up their pagan occupiers and sort out the heretics next door. They can't for a moment comprehend that God's judgement might involve flinging open the door and ushering all those outsiders in.

Jesus also knows that people are making misjudgements about him – opinions rooted in fear – that will lead to his death, in which he will willingly offer himself because nothing less will make us sit up and heed what he's trying to tell us about divine judgement, always tempered by mercy, drenched in a level of loving acceptance that goes beyond human comprehension. Anthony de Mello writes:

> Our value does not come from what we have done. Rather it comes from the Father's Love. That is where all our value comes from. That is where our salvation comes from (1 John 4:7–12)! This is such a very forceful statement that you could put it in psychological terms. Jesus is saying: Do not be defensive. Accept the fact that you have inadequacies and fears, and that you have a lot to grow. Then you will change.[6]

But it's so tempting to demand that people change first before we lift the velvet rope to offer access to communion, membership or fellowship. 'Become like us,' we say, 'and then we'll confer God's approval on you.' So much of church life is cloaked in the myth of middle-class respectability. Churches are only an expression of the kingdom when they're full of people who, rather than being pleased with themselves, know that they fall short of perfection but accept the king's invitation to the banquet regardless. It's not our outer behaviour that matters, nor presenting ourselves in ways humans deem respectable. It's simply our willingness to say 'yes' to the invitation and join in with the feast and the dancing. If your table manners are a bit rough or you dance like your Granddad, it doesn't matter, just so long as you're joining in. It's your openness to allowing God's Spirit to work in you that brings about transformation, not putting on a show for the sniffy ladies in the hats or the scowling churchwarden.

We've come down a very long road of church history that's allowed an accretion of Christian judgementalism to overlay the way we do church, developing a matching theology to justify it. If you Google 'What did Jesus say about judging others?' some of the top hits are bloggers asserting their right to set others straight.

I attended a funeral recently at which the minister preached on Luke 13.22–30, where it says:

> Jesus went through one town and village after another, teaching as he made his way to Jerusalem. Someone asked him, 'Lord, will only a few be saved?' He said to them, 'Strive to enter through the narrow door; for many, I tell you, will try to enter and will not be able. When once the owner of the house has got up and shut the door, and you begin to stand outside and to knock at the door, saying, "Lord, open to us", then in reply he will say to you, "I do not know where you come from." Then you will begin to say, "We ate and drank with you, and you taught in our streets." But he will say, "I do not know where you come from; go away from me, all you evildoers!" There will be weeping and gnashing of teeth when you see Abraham and Isaac and Jacob and all the

prophets in the kingdom of God, and you yourselves thrown out. Then people will come from east and west, from north and south, and will eat in the kingdom of God. Indeed, some are last who will be first, and some are first who will be last.'

The minister's message to the congregation of mourners that morning was, 'Open your heart to Jesus before it's too late because one day he'll slam the door in your face.' In other words, 'We're Jesus' in-crowd and you can be in too if you hurry. If you don't, you'll be punished for it.' The open invitation to join the great feast has been turned into a threat, rooted in self-righteousness and used to coerce people into faith.

As Tom Wright puts it: 'We should be cautious about lifting this passage out and applying it directly to the larger question of eternal salvation. Jesus' urgent warnings to his own contemporaries were aimed at the particular emergency they then faced.'[7]

Jesus' made-to-shock rhetoric is in the context of his consistent message that the religious leaders of God's chosen people, so contemptuous of Gentiles and satisfied in themselves, are being too slow to respond to God's message. At this rate the Gentiles will end up in the kingdom of God before they do. It's all part of his mission to break down barriers and divisions between people and open up God's invitation to all.

We've had 2,000 years of furious bricklaying to build those walls right back up again. Never mind Jew and Gentile, now we've neatly sectioned off Catholic from Protestant, evangelical from liberal, charismatic from liturgical, Western Church from Eastern Orthodox and so on.

The radically inclusive nature of Christ's invitation doesn't fit the command-and-control approach to evangelism still very evident in some church traditions. Jesus says 'Woe to you . . . For you have taken away the key of knowledge; you did not enter yourselves, and you hindered those who were entering' (Luke 11.52). In Matthew 23, Jesus lets rip on religious hypocrisy, issuing a sevenfold indictment of scribes and Pharisees. Religion that's self-serving, without compassion or doesn't reach out to the poor is not of the kingdom that Christ has come to usher in.

Christ's judgement of us is an ongoing daily experience, if we allow the light of the presence of God to illuminate our inner life and show it up for what it really is, 'the best of me, which may well be not what I am proud of, and the worst of me, which is not what it has occurred to me to be ashamed of'.[8] As we grow in this self-understanding we move forward in our journey towards holiness, becoming more forgiving towards ourselves and more tolerant towards others.

Then we might be ready to rip the church doors off their hinges and allow the rest of the sinners in, before shouting, 'Let's party!'

# *Part 3*

# TOWARDS DISCERNMENT

———◆·◆·◆———

'Do not judge by appearances, but judge with right
judgement.'

*John 7.24*

# 13

## *Getting at the truth*

———•◦•———

Bountiful God, giver of all gifts,
who poured your Spirit upon your servant Barnabas
and gave him grace to encourage others:
help us, by his example,
to be generous in our judgements
and unselfish in our service.[1]

Every day we have to use our critical faculties to make sense of
the world around us and the new opportunities and challenges
it presents. We might have to adjudicate on a squabble among
our children, colleagues or congregation. Is the person in front
of you telling the truth, a version of it or the opposite of it? Does
the person begging for money really want my cash to buy a square
meal or his next fix? Which politician's promises should I trust
and give my vote to? Is the article I'm reading accurate or reflecting the bias of the journalist who wrote it? Why are my neighbours
passing on this gossip – what's their agenda? Making judgements
might also be part of your job: investigating bullying, a breach of
discipline or a crime.

But as we have seen, our capacity to make wise judgements may
be distorted by our own psychological biases or the limits of our
experience – we may even have a concrete agenda to undermine
somebody or at the very least justify ourselves.

The judgements we make of other people help us navigate how
we relate to them as individuals as well as to society as a whole.
Many of these assessments are driven by the question: 'Can I trust
you?' Trust not only grows out of relationships as they deepen but
can be a gift we choose to offer someone. At the same time, snap

judgements, suspicion and scepticism are all obstacles to good relating. Yet we can't be naive and enter every encounter unthinkingly. How do we tread the fine line Jesus called 'right judgement?' In this final part of the book I want to try and find a route through these tensions. What practical steps can we take to ensure our judgements are fair? How can we cultivate a spirituality that helps us relate to people as Jesus did? How do we discern well in a critical age?

I'm a great fan of film and, as such, rely on the advice of film critics to help me decide which movies I make the effort to go and see, which to ignore. Perhaps the UK's greatest film critic in my lifetime was Philip French. He wrote on the subject of film for *The Observer* newspaper for 50 years, before retiring as the paper's chief film critic on his eightieth birthday. The American film director Martin Scorsese said in tribute to him:

> When you make a movie, it's nice to be appreciated. But it's genuinely heartening, and rare, to be understood. Whenever I read Philip French's elegant and thoughtful criticism, I felt like I was in the company of someone who not only loved cinema but who felt a sense of responsibility toward it as an art form. His knowledge of movies is vast – all kinds of movies, and I remember that he had a special fondness for genre pictures and for the work of Walter Hill and others – and he has always been very generous about sharing it with his readers. I want to say that his criticism, taken altogether, has ennobled cinema, the people who create it and the people who love it. Like his many devoted readers, I'm sorry that he's retiring. The man is irreplaceable.[2]

There is much in Scorsese's remarks that help us see what set French apart from other critics who superficially carp or slag off movies they don't enjoy. He had immense knowledge and experience of the subject. According to Mark Kermode, his successor on *The Observer*, a film critic should first 'accurately describe a film and then ascribe it to the right school of film, before mentioning its tangential connections to other films'.[3] Knowledge of the subject and experience of the field gives weight and authority to judgement. But French also brought an empathy to the process; he was a critical friend. His reviews became compelling reading for film fans, who respected his depth of knowledge and ability to place a movie in the context of its wider genre. To inform his critiques he brought a level of experience most readers lacked. It was never simply a question of whether he liked a film or not, or whether he judged it good or bad, although you'd usually be clear on those points by the end of the review. I also liked the fact that his reviews, unlike most others these days, didn't grade films between one and five stars. You had to read the whole article to understand his opinion, a practice that refused to pander to our liking for snap judgements.

When it comes to film criticism it's easy to see exactly what qualified Philip French to judge – someone with immense experience in the field who could not only bring that knowledge to bear but had a seat high above the landscape that allowed him to take in more of the vista than most others. Our judgements should be informed – in part, as we've already seen, by a self-awareness of our limitations and prejudices but also by a body of knowledge about the subject of our judgement. How often do we see people make judgements about immigrants, asylum seekers, bankers, prisoners, welfare claimants, homosexuals, politicians and so on, without ever having *really* got to know any?

Reading the published diaries of the legendary socialist MP Tony Benn, I was struck by his remarkable curiosity. Time and again he gives an account of conversations he struck up with people he encountered in everyday life, such as an immigrant driving a taxi. 'Where are you from?' 'What brought you here?' 'Do you have family?' 'Can you make ends meet driving taxis?' These regular enquiring conversations helped Benn build up a knowledge of the issues ordinary people faced, the better to represent their interests in parliament. (Contrast this with another former MP who, upon getting into a taxi recently, started a dispute with the driver over the quickest route to take. To assert his claim to being better fitted to judge on this point, he said, 'You've been driving a cab for ten years. I've been in the Cabinet. I'm an award-winning broadcaster. I'm a Queen's Counsel. You think that your experiences are anything compared to mine?' I think I know which one I'd trust to get me home in time for cocoa.)

In the legal world there are different types of judges. In the UK, as in the USA, our judges preside over a ding-dong between opposing counsel before pronouncing judgment over who's made the best case. In France, so I believe, the judge's job is to sift through all the evidence to discern the truth – a system based much more on enquiry. The adversarial nature of our system hasn't always led to justice or the full facts of a case coming to light. And there are some very real questions currently being asked about how appropriate it is for, say, traumatized victims of sexual abuse to be cross-examined by barristers hell-bent on discrediting their testimony or character.

Within church life, building a case for your opinion by knocking down the arguments of others is no less present, but I question whether it nurtures the spirit of love we should be cultivating with our brothers and sisters.

Christians get most vexed about issues of heresy and orthodoxy – as they did in the times of the early Church. In Acts 24, Paul is accused of 'heresy', as the King James Version puts it (v. 14) – more coyly translated as belonging to a 'sect' in modern translations such as NRSV. As Malcolm Guite points out, it's somewhat ironic that the key architect of Christian theology, whom all sides cite when accusing each other of heresy, is himself accused of the very same thing:

> One might have hoped that this episode would have given every subsequent controversialist pause before they drew breath to anathematise one another. Indeed, Paul's very phrasing – 'that way which they call heresy' – draws our attention to the fact that 'heresy' is always an adversarial, and not an objective, definition. That is not to say that there isn't an ultimate truth, and that some people will turn out to have been right and others wrong. But it is to say that all our present definitions are necessarily partial and partisan, and that now, in this present life, we need a certain humility before the truth, a certain courtesy towards one another.[4]

Getting at theological truth is a tricky business and necessitates an acknowledgement that even our most cherished religious beliefs are hampered by the limits of our humanity.

I've been rather heartened by a book called *The Meaning of Jesus* by N. T. Wright and the late Marcus Borg.[5] The writers are both biblical scholars but from very different church traditions and theologies. They also happened to be great friends, and wrote their book rooted in a practice of praying together. The book examines different aspects of Jesus – the authors both write a chapter about each topic covered and explain how they understand it from their particular theological perspective. There's much they don't agree on (and plenty they do), but they've transcended the need to belittle each other, simply presenting their differing views side by side. The ultimate truth, I'm sure, won't be represented solely in the writing of the traditionalist or the liberal but found across both at different points in the book. It's as if the authors have presented us with all the evidence so that we can sift through it ourselves and be enriched by the wider vista offered.

The Church could learn much from such an approach. It's perhaps similar to what Archbishop Justin Welby calls 'disagreeing well', and is certainly different from, for example, the spectacle – certainly at the last Lambeth Conference – of archbishops absenting themselves from receiving Holy Communion alongside fellow primates with whom they disagree. 'For now we see in a mirror, dimly, but then we will see face to face. Now I know only in part; then I will know fully, even as I have been fully known' (1 Corinthians 13.12). Being mindful of our limited perspective is always prudent when feeling tempted to burn bridges.

Similarly, it troubled me at theological college that ministerial training adopted the argumentative mode of academic study. It was never enough for an essay to demonstrate a knowledge of the variety of thinking about the given issue in hand. An argument always had to be made by attacking one scholar's view in order to shore up another's. I can see how this approach would be important in the evidence-based world of scientific research. I'm far from convinced it's appropriate for students preparing to preach a gospel of reconciliation and the unity of the body of Christ.

Academic tutors are often an opinionated and argumentative bunch, quick to attack the views of others – a trait unfortunately observable in many clergy. I wonder where they learned that?

What, then, is the alternative to the destructiveness of much of our judgementalism? Because, of course, we do still need to navigate and assess difficult or conflicting issues presented to us. To help us think about what 'right judgement' might mean, I'd like to offer an alternative word to help us disassociate our thinking from the sort of toxic judgementalism we've been considering up until now.

That word is *discernment*. This isn't, of course, a new word for many, and has a long and particular use within Christian spirituality. Nonetheless I think it serves us well as a counterpoint to judgementalism. Discernment implies less of a snap judgement and more the kind of inquiring, informed, generous, prayerful and rooted consideration that is the polar opposite to self-justifying, ego-driven judgementalism.

How, then, do we discern well?

# 14

## Discernment

———•◆•———

### Humility

'All of you must clothe yourselves with humility in your dealings with one another, for "God opposes the proud, but gives grace to the humble"' (1 Peter 5.5).

Discernment begins with humility.

There are plenty of false notions about humility – that it's a sort of pious modesty one puts on, a willingness to roll over and be someone else's doormat or allowing ourselves to wallow in our shortcomings. Perhaps some people's humility is (mis)interpreted by others as looking a bit like that.

Humility is actually an *accepting honesty* about ourselves, to ourselves. It's grounded in the reality of who we truly are, being truthful about our strengths and our weaknesses. A great deal of human behaviour is characterized by a pretence that we're better, smarter or more in control than we actually are. Humility dispenses with these and tries to become a bit more honest.

For some of us it swings too far the other way, constantly putting ourselves down or being unbearably self-deprecating. That's not authentic either because it denies the reality of our strengths. Humility is comfortable with the idea that we're good at some things, gifted even. It doesn't feel the need to brag about them or big ourselves up, just simply accept them. And equally, we can adopt a reality about our limitations – in knowledge, experience, skills and so on. This is just me. This is who I am. In that state we navigate life – and our relationships with others – in a very different way from 'the great pretence'.

'Let the same mind be in you that was in Christ Jesus,' wrote the apostle Paul to the church in Philippi (Philippians 2.5). This doesn't mean we all become assimilated into the divine, losing our capacity for independent thought and reason (I'm imagining the Borg here, for any *Star Trek* geeks out there). Nor that we ought always agree with each other: why would we, when each of us only sees a part of the whole picture?

For Paul, taking on the mind of Christ was an active exercise – working hard to live out our lives in the same self-emptying way as Christ, something we can only do when we spend plenty of time steeped in the gospel and in prayer. Paul was writing to a divided and squabbling Church (sound familiar?), and urged them to become more Christlike. Malcolm Guite writes:

> As we stare across the divide between conservative and liberal, tradition and fresh expression, North and South, can we find enough encouragement in what we share, enough compassion and sympathy, enough consolation from the Love we all acknowledge, to stop clinging to an identity that depends on being against some heretical 'other', and become instead parts of the bridge that Love wants to build between us?[1]

In the same letter Paul also writes, 'Do nothing from selfish ambition or conceit, but in humility regard others as better than yourselves. Let each of you look not to your own interests, but to the interests of others' (Philippians 2.3–4). Following Christ's injunction to 'love your neighbour as yourself', Paul seems to be offering a practical tip for managing that. Instead of imagining ourselves superior to others, why not try imagining others superior to us and see how that alters attitudes and behaviour towards them? We know, of course, that in God's eyes we're all equal – the dualistic comparison of better and worse is not how we're loved. But Paul, I think, recognizes that we might need to play a psychological trick on ourselves to overcome our tendency to look down on others. If we condition ourselves to look up to them instead, perhaps we'll be better able to serve them and keep their interests in mind.

However, we must find ways of doing this that break the constant cycle of comparing ourselves to others, and develop a spiritual mastery that moves us into a different mindset. The letter of James, for example, urges us to be impartial in our dealings with others (James 2.9). Treating others according to their supposed status relative to oneself should have no place in church, or indeed elsewhere in life.

Humility is a starting point for discernment because it shifts us off our self-erected pedestals from which we're tempted to judge others. If we see people instead as equals, view them as *essentially good*, we can come to understand them from a very different starting point.

## Goodness in others

Everyone is made in the image of God. Remembering this reminds me that we're all fundamentally good at our core. When we see goodness in ourselves and those around us, we begin to expect it more, to see it more often in others and look for ways to nurture it within ourselves. However, if we believe people are essentially bad then we expect bad behaviour, become more judgemental and intolerant, fearful even.

Different Christian traditions emphasize goodness and sinfulness in different ways. A theology that stresses that we're rotten to our marrow and deserve damnation easily lapses into intolerant fundamentalism. Why wouldn't it? Everyone around you is evil and self-centred, cruel and vicious. This cultivates fear and an urge to shelter ourselves in churches where we can separate ourselves off from the 'sinners'.

A theology based on goodness starts in the garden of Eden, not at the point at which the first humans sin but earlier in the narrative. God's creation of humankind is the last act of creation, after which God sits back and takes a good, long hard look at '*everything* that he had made, and indeed, it was *very good*' (Genesis 1.31; emphasis added). Goodness is woven into the divine project. God's love for humanity leads to our being given free will. Sometimes we choose to deviate from what God desires for us. The self-centredness within us pulls us away from the divine at our core, but it doesn't remove it – God's faithfulness and steadfastness and being-ever-present-to-us mean that we can't dislodge the goodness in us. Desmond Tutu and Mpho Tutu write:

> [I]f we are fundamentally good, we simply need to redis-cover this true nature and act accordingly. This insight into our essential goodness has shifted how I interact with other people; it has even shaken how I read the Bible.
>
> Goodness changes the way we see the world, the way we see others, the way we see ourselves. The way we see ourselves matters. It affects how we treat people.[2]

When we believe there's goodness in others, we'll begin to make an effort to look for it. If we view strangers as potential friends rather than probable threats, we're more likely to search for the signs of goodness within them, to reach out the hand of friend-ship. And when people whose faces don't fit walk into our church, whose lifestyle could be a bit more stable or who wear the scars of their upbringing in their behaviour towards others, perhaps we can pause to search for the goodness within them rather than jump to conclusions. God sometimes glimmers in the lives of our most broken members of society – if we only trouble to see it. (I've had, for example, some of the wisest and most insightful conversa-tions with people who were quite seriously mentally ill.)

Humility is a great leveller because it means being real about ourselves (basically good, but a bit limited and screwed up in places) and about other people (basically good, but a bit limited and screwed up in places). The trick is to seek out the goodness and let go of the need to obsess about the limitations and screwed-upness. David Lonsdale writes:

> It is not always recognized that discernment lies at the heart of Christian spirituality . . . Trying to be a Christian means learning how to respond with love to God, to people and to circumstances. It means searching for ways of living out the two great gospel commandments of loving God and our neigh-bour, while recognizing the imperfection of our attempts.[3]

The path from judgementalism to discernment begins with noticing when we're being judgemental, and breaking the pattern. We watch our minds for judgemental thoughts and alert ourselves before we build them up into a great self-justifying narrative. You might try wearing an elastic band on your wrist, and snap it whenever you find yourself making a rash judgement about someone. Or you could pinch yourself or click your fingers – some physical response that helps burst the bubble of the thought developing in your mind. Then you can begin to reframe your thinking, to see Christ in those before you, pray for them or project love towards them.

When a friend of mine was in the process of quitting cigarettes, he read up on all the bad effects of smoking, while continuing to smoke. The method he followed – successfully I might add – encouraged him to give attention to the moment he drew on the cigarette. Instead of absent-mindedly going through the motions, he developed a kind of mindfulness about it. What he noticed by doing this was that the 'hit' he told himself he couldn't live without was actually rather boring.

When I lash out in judgement it may seem satisfying in the moment. As we cultivate an attentiveness to what is happening in the mind we begin to see how ungratifying it actually is, because of course it is a false comfort, temporary and illusory – and it has a long-term damaging effect on both our relationships and our integrity.

## Curiosity

A number of years ago, when you could still take a fast boat from Folkestone to Boulogne-sur-Mer, my friend Rob and I decided we'd go on a day trip. After lunch, as we wandered the narrow cobbled streets, we called into the Basilica of Notre-Dame de Boulogne. The building has an impressive dome that dominates the town's skyline, although I don't remember anything particularly remarkable about the interior. As in many Roman Catholic churches, there were cubicles to enable the clergy to hear confessions in confidence. I pulled aside the curtain of one to have a sneaky peek. Stashed inside were bits of old carpet and some other junk, underneath a sign that read, in several languages, 'Curiosity is a sin.' Caught red-handed, I laughed out loud.

But I couldn't disagree more. Curiosity is essential in loving our neighbour. It's in our capacity to put ourselves in others' shoes, or to be enquiring about their words and actions, that we become better at seeing things from their perspectives. Curiosity counteracts our instinct for snap judgements by bearing in mind that there's always more to learn and in taking time to explore and understand a situation more.

One of the qualities of someone you'd describe as a 'people person' is that they make you feel they're on your side and take time to understand you. Some of us hold back from doing this because we fear being thought of as nosy. There's certainly a big difference between a naturally empathic curiosity and an interest driven by a sort of gossipy need-to-know. People can tell which you are from the way you ask or phrase your questions.

Nurturing our curiosity can also extend to how we seek to inform ourselves about issues that fall outside our experience. It's always fruitful to avoid relying on the casual opinions of colleagues or friends and seek out authoritative sources. It's easy to take for granted what a friend tells you as fact, without remembering that the friend may be ill-informed, prejudiced or conditioned by the agenda of a newspaper. We must seek out those with real experience of an issue. And when dealing with individuals, taking time to understand their experience spins a conversation in a very different way from trying to project *our* life experience onto *their* circumstances.

Learning to ask openly phrased questions and cultivate listening skills would be good topics for congregations to study together. There's so much potential for churches to become places that exercise a form of hospitality based, in St Francis' words, on 'seeking to understand rather than be understood'.[4] We're sometimes very good at the tea and cake bit of hospitality, and in a crisis people will often rally round to offer a listening ear, a shoulder to cry on or pop round with a casserole. Yet a great deal of church life manages successfully to bypass a genuine understanding of what's going on in the lives of others, or the past experiences that have shaped them as people.

We get so caught up in the busyness of *doing church* that we forget to give attention to each other. Clergy can be as guilty of this as anyone, with the oft-cited hectic schedule used as a defence against properly engaging with people. The increasing managerialism imposed by church structures doesn't help, and we need to cultivate new ways of creating an environment where people can be properly communicative.

One organization I know starts its meetings by simply offering time for everyone to say how they are. No, not that polite 'I'm fine thank you' that we all do when we're going though the motions. I'm talking about being real. Nobody is forced to speak, but others remain silent when a member of the group is talking. It's a very effective way of tuning in to each other and understanding what everyone's carrying with them.

This takes time, not least in building up the necessary degree of trust within the group. Indeed anything that involves creating better understanding between people is time consuming. For some it will be such a different way of relating that it might require several attempts before they become accustomed to it. Practices like this push us to change the way we listen to one another, inviting us to engage in ways that explore what we can learn from others rather than what we might tell them.

I've begun to notice how some of my clergy colleagues communicate. Conversations about how things are in, say, my parish quickly lead to their giving me advice or offering solutions – often without really taking time to understand the situation. They ask no questions but offer lots of answers for misconceived problems. This is another way judgementalism is felt. There's no curiosity, just a drive to fix things. I sense the way these conversations flow, bearing down on me in a somewhat oppressive fashion rather than being inquiring, listening deeply or helping to open up the issues I'm trying to express.

We clergy should know better, given our job is not just to *do* but also to *be*. Pastoral care is about getting alongside people and entering into their experience with them. This is the incarnation at work within us. It's certainly not at work in us if we perceive ourselves to be divine troubleshooters, popping up to put things right for people.

We do, I hope, manage to avoid being like this when dealing with death, where we know nothing we can say will fix the profound feelings of grief and loss a family may be feeling. Simply spending time accompanying them through that, with a willingness to listen – or perhaps just sit in silence – is tremendously supportive. It's not having answers that matters, but a willingness to pitch up and be present. Some of us are a bit slower to recognize that this is the mode in which we could operate in lots of other situations too, not just around funerals. There's a tremendous pressure sometimes to feel we must have solutions to offer rather than a ready willingness to explore a situation properly. When I'm prepared to be honest about my limitations I become a much better priest because I simply start asking questions. Quite often in the conversation that ensues we'll figure out a way forward together. And sometimes we won't and just offer it to God in prayer. This is what *being* means – entering a situation with a simple openness to experiencing it rather than trying to fix it.

This isn't just a job for clergy, this is for all of us, working to create churches that flourish based on mutual understanding and self-giving. We can't always get it right and sometimes we just have to weave the flaws into the whole piece. But if we're committed to creating churches where hospitality is about real engagement with each other, then this is a project worth pursuing.

The way of discernment maintains an openness to the situations and people we encounter. We ask rather than tell, seek to learn rather than fix. Our engagement with others is more a matter of invitation than imposition. As Sam Wells suggests, the call to engage with others is about what we can learn from them, not what we can give them.[5]

But what happens when we're trying to get along with people with whom we have deep and profound disagreements?

## *New ways to dialogue*

Christians squabble about many things, but perhaps nothing has proved more divisive in recent years than changing social attitudes to homosexuality. With the advent of civil partnerships and equal marriage, the Church is struggling to reach consensus about how to respond. Much of the discord isn't about human sexuality per se but more how this issue exposes underlying fault lines in our different theologies and approaches to interpreting Scripture. Different traditions are fighting to preserve the way they understand and practise their faith.

A number of years ago my deanery in north London invited each of its churches to send a representative to participate in a 'civil discourse' about homosexuality. Over the course of a year or so we met once a month. The rules were simple: each evening two members of the group would talk about their experience of the subject and how they'd come to form their views on it. No one was to interrupt or offer their opinion on anything they heard, but when each person had finished speaking there was a time for the group to ask questions – not point-scoring inquiries but curiosity-driven exploratory questions, designed to unpack what that speaker had shared. The group took time to check it understood what each person had said.

This approach was profoundly effective because it bypassed judgementalism. No one could jump in and disagree or start trying to undermine another's position. In spite of the wide spectrum of views represented within the group, there were no arguments and no heated moments – none. Everybody understood the ground rules from the start. We each knew that we'd not only get our turn to be heard but that the group would listen to us in an unusually deep way. Their job as listeners was to help each speaker express themselves as clearly and fully as possible.

Did anyone change their mind about homosexuality as a result of the civil discourse? I don't believe so. But the antagonism that's often felt when people with opposing views get together never materialized. We ended the process with a sense of unity, of 'disagreeing well', to borrow Archbishop Welby's term again. There was no casual dismissal of others as bigots or backsliders. Having listened deeply to each other we understood what had informed each person's position. We may not have reached the same conclusion ourselves but it was easier to respect people with opposing views having taken time to understand them. There was a softening of language in the way people expressed themselves because we were never put on the defensive. Each evening we'd enter into the experience of others, get alongside them and walk in their shoes for a while.

When Christ became one of us he entered fully into the human experience, as 'one who in every respect has been tested as we are' (Hebrews 4.15). His judgement is tempered by mercy rooted in the incarnational experience of undergoing life as we have. As our judge he is able to 'sympathize with our weaknesses'. This is *empathy* at work – an ability to understand deeply what others are experiencing. The more informed we are about another person's perspective, the better able we are to see the sense in it.

Now I may be tempted to judge people who've developed drug or alcohol problems as having shown poor self-discipline or made bad choices. They've got themselves into a right mess and have no one but themselves to blame. When I talk to them and hear, say, a story of childhood neglect or abuse, I might do better at getting alongside them. They'll still need to acknowledge they have a problem and take responsibility for moving out of it, but an understanding friend – albeit with some firmness at times – will do a better job of supporting them than high-handed judgement-alism, which seldom dares to roll up its sleeves and get stuck in. Judgement is a way of avoiding engagement, while empathy walks right in.

## Empathy

Empathy isn't the same as sympathy, which presents no challenge to the recipients but simply expresses sadness at how they're feeling. Empathy requires wisdom, and goes hand in hand with discernment. The willingness to understand what others are going through doesn't mean we have to collude with their inter-pretation of their circumstances. We can challenge them on some of that. Most folk can cope with being called out on something they've said, provided they feel an attempt has been made to understand them first. Judgementalism, on the other hand, simply antagonizes.

I was discussing this book with a clergy colleague. 'We've got to tell people their lives are out of order sometimes, surely?' he said. Perhaps – but it shouldn't be our first response. The Church's misguided divine prerogative to set others straight has been so damaging and alienating. I find in most pastoral conversations that people already know what their problems are – and they don't need a finger wagged at them. On rarer occasions they may need a reality check, which can be better offered when we've spent time alongside them, getting to know and understand their circumstances properly. The way of discernment takes time to make sure our insight is well informed before saying, something like: 'I think the problem might be ........ What do you think?'; 'I notice a repeating pattern here. Why do you think that is?'; 'You said before you were going to try and do ........ What happened?'

Rudyard Kipling wrote:

> I keep six honest serving-men
> (They taught me all I knew);
> Their names are What and Why and When
> And How and Where and Who.[6]

Any openly phrased question will start with one of Kipling's servants. Questions that are leading or phrased in a closed way begin with words like 'did', 'do', 'does', 'is', 'shall', 'was', 'can', 'would' and so on, and are to be avoided unless we're checking our understanding of something the other has said – 'Did you mean ....... ?' Just because our questions remain open and curious doesn't mean they have to flinch from exploring the hard stuff. True humility is open to being put right, but when we're shoring ourselves up with delusions about ourselves then direct admonishment comes as a threat. (Indeed one could argue that we've lost a constructive practice of admonishment these days.) A questioning approach allows us a way in to those harder conversations without putting people on the back foot.

The apostle Paul, ever full of good advice, writes: 'My friends, if anyone is detected in a transgression, you who have received the Spirit should restore such a one in a spirit of gentleness' (Galatians 6.1). This is a letter in which the apostle is trying to navigate the clashing cultures of Jews and Gentiles within church life. As ever with our theology, we need to join the dots and make sure one piece of teaching isn't taken out of context to contradict others. Paul recognizes that in church life there may be moments where we need to help each other back on course. We do so, however, mindful of the way Christ dealt with people's shortcomings. For him there was none of the power-crazed control-freakery or 'heavy shepherding' some churches have made it their mission to practise.

When we teach our people humility, exhibit it ourselves and extend hospitality in a way that seeks to understand, when we walk in their shoes with empathy, then yes: a space might open up from time to time where restoring someone in a spirit of gentleness would be appropriate. But notice how much groundwork there is to do first.

Rather than condemn others for not living up to our expectations, it's more constructive to determine what their objectives are. This is a question actors ask when taking on a new role. 'What does my character want to get out of this situation?' It's very hard to play a role authentically if you make a judgement about your character, so actors find neutral ways of describing the qualities and characteristics of the person they'll play: 'She's ambitious [rather than 'bossy']'; 'He's disappointed [rather than 'bitter']'; 'She's consolidating her power [rather than 'scheming and manipulative']'. Thinking in this way allows the actor to get inside the character's head and really understand what it is she or he wants to achieve. It strikes me as a useful strategy for lots of situations in life.

Ignatius of Loyola had something similar in mind when he developed his rule of Presupposition. 'Beware of condemning anyone's action. Consider your neighbour's intention, which is often honest and innocent, even though the act seems bad in outward appearance.' James Martin writes:

> Ignatius says we 'ought to be more eager to put a good interpretation on a neighbor's statement than to condemn it.'
>
> Always give people the benefit of the doubt. What's more, says Ignatius, if you're not sure what a person means, you

should . . . 'ask how the other means it' . . . We expect others to judge us according to our *intentions*, but we judge others according to their actions . . . In other words, we say to ourselves, *My intention was good. Why don't they see this?* But when it comes to other people, we often fail to give them the benefit of the doubt. We say, 'Look what they did!'

The Presupposition also helps us remember the other person's intention, which helps ground relationships in openness. You approach every interaction with an open heart and mind by presuming – even when it's hard to do – that the other person is doing his or her best and isn't out to get you.[7]

There's something in empathy that doesn't expect perfection from others because it recognizes that none of us is perfect. 'If your heart is gentle,' wrote Francis de Sales, 'your judgements will be gentle; if it is loving, so will your judgements be.'[8]

I find this very hard to swallow. I've been a harsh critic of the Church and its inadequacies for very many years. My greatest judgements have been about how the Church fails to live up to the radical nature of the gospel – just as I do, in fact. I'm embarrassed by the behaviour and beliefs of fellow Christians and often anxious to avoid being associated with them.

The prophet Ezekiel spoke these prophetic words from God: 'A new heart I will give you, and a new spirit I will put within you; and I will remove from your body the heart of stone and give you a heart of flesh' (Ezekiel 36.26). Bring it on!

Dietrich Bonhoeffer wrote that the Church is a gift of God:

Just as [Christians] should not be constantly feeling [their] spiritual pulse, so, too, the Christian community has not been given to us by God for us to be constantly taking its temperature. The more thankfully we daily receive what is given to us, the more surely and steadily will fellowship increase and grow from day to day as God pleases.[9]

This view of fellowship challenges my judgementalism and pushes me towards practising gratitude instead.

## Practising gratitude

Paul wrote to the early church in Thessalonica: 'Rejoice always, pray without ceasing, give thanks in all circumstances; for this is the will of God in Christ Jesus for you. Do not quench the Spirit' (1 Thessalonians 5.16–19). For Paul, nurturing the Spirit of God within ourselves and others meant looking for the good, giving thanks for the positives, taking note of the gifts around us and putting gratitude for them at the heart of our prayers.

If we're constantly grumbling or the only time we pray is to ask God for something, it becomes harder to maintain a spirituality that sustains us. Prayer becomes self-serving, all about me and not much about God, who we treat like a divine Santa Claus, hoping that whatever we want will be dished out provided we've been good. But when our prayers begin in thanksgiving we re-orientate our minds towards the love God pours on us. We count our blessings and reframe how we see our lives. There's something about being in a thankful state of mind that's motivating and energizing.

Gratitude is a key strand of Christian spirituality and indeed of some other faiths too. Psychologists tell us that practising gratitude is good for our health and well-being, as well as our relationships. Why wouldn't it be? Being around joyful people is so much better than being around people who constantly carp and complain.

Prayers of thanksgiving are a way of joining in with the eternal song of praise, adding our chorus to the heavenly hosts. This is how we weave earthly living into eternal life. But how do we follow Paul's instruction to rejoice always? Christians have developed a number of approaches to this, but I want to highlight just one.

Five hundred years ago Ignatius of Loyola developed a set of spiritual exercises that have, over the centuries, helped many Christians deepen their relationship with God. One such exercise is called the 'Examen', a contemplative practice for use morning and evening. And it starts with gratitude. James Martin again:

You recall the good things that happened to you during the day, and you give thanks for any 'benefits' . . .

Ignatius meant 'benefits' in the broadest possible sense. Obvious things would include any good news, a tender moment with a [loved one], finishing an important project at work. But also less-obvious things: the surprising sight of sunlight on the pavement in the middle of a bleak midwinter's day, the taste of a ham-and-cheese sandwich you had for lunch, satisfaction at the end of a tiring day spent caring for your children.

For Ignatius many things – no matter how seemingly inconsequential – are occasions for gratitude. You recall them and you 'relish' or 'savor' them, as he would say.[10]

This conscious effort to acknowledge our daily benefits before God can have a very powerful effect. When I use the Examen I find myself looking out for things in the course of the day I can include in my list of benefits – it becomes a kind of unceasing prayer. And it's a very powerful antidote to my usual habit of stocktaking all the little irritations and hiccups encountered in the day. In the same way that grumbling about life's little difficulties makes me more aware and obsessive about them, practising gratitude begins to build a continual awareness of God as the source of all goodness and love. The light of Christ within us blazes more brightly. It's the very opposite of the Spirit being quenched.

Recognizing that some things in life bring us desolation rather than consolation – not least the mistakes we've made or the moments we've let ourselves down – is also part of the Examen. But it always begins with seeking God's grace and practising gratitude.

We do this in our worship together, of course. The celebration of Holy Communion is one great act of thanksgiving to God for the reconciliation brought to us through the cross of Christ. But I don't believe for a moment that Paul was thinking about formal services of worship when he instructed the Thessalonians to rejoice always and give thanks in all circumstances. This is for *all* of our common life together: the conversations we have over coffee after church; the deliberations at meetings; the way we work together to organize events and activities. Our conduct should be conditioned by ceaseless gratitude rather than endless grumbling.

Paul's advice to rejoice always and give thanks in all circumstances wasn't directed at individuals. He was writing to a church to instruct them on their life together as a community of faith. Lucy Lind Hogan writes:

> They are all to rejoice. And when? Not at a particular time, nor only in good times, but always. They are to pray always. They are to give thanks not just for the good things that happen to them, but 'in all circumstances.'[11]

Like the Church today, the Thessalonians had their worries. But Paul doesn't want their collective life together to be shaped by their anxiety, rather a commonly held spirit of thanksgiving to God for all the goodness and love they receive. So too for us. Paul's words ring down through the centuries as true and clear as the day he wrote them, for it's a message we need to hold on to now as much as ever.

The path from judgement to discernment, then, lies in a life that practises ceaseless *gratitude*, while being grounded in *humility*, orientated towards *goodness* and exercising a deep *empathy* towards others. These are the prisms through which we begin to regard and relate to others differently – they are the way of love.

# 15

## Prophetic witness

---

### Valuing reflection over opinions

Our opinions are powerful stuff. As every superhero will tell you, you must use your powers wisely. With the emergence of online social media, opinions have become a social currency on Twitter, Facebook and so on. One of my New Year resolutions this year was to deactivate my Facebook account. It's often said by those who shun social networks that they're not interested in reading what people had for lunch, when they've chipped a fingernail or missed their bus. Personally I didn't encounter too many posts about the dreary minutiae of people's lives. No, what turned me off was something else entirely.

I'd noticed how people's posts had changed from sharing their news to broadcasting opinions on a vast range of subjects. I became rather fed up with being battered by this daily salvo of dogma and the implicit invitation to collude by 'liking' such posts. And of course we assume affirmation when lots of people click the 'like' button on something we've posted. I found myself feeling less connected to people who presented a regular challenge to agree or disagree with them – it became an antisocial network, not least given how poor a forum it is for proper, informed, debate.

Nobody wants depth on social media. We want to grasp what others are saying instantly so we can decide whether we approve or not. Judgementalism is part of the fun, but I soon began to find it boring and, occasionally, upsetting. Now this isn't a polemic against social networks, we just need to be aware that they can lead to a hollow sense of validation, built on how others respond to whatever we post. Without face to face interaction there isn't the same dynamic that allows us to engage properly with one another, check out the responses or body language of the other or modify our tone based on who might be reading. It becomes harder to sense when someone has misunderstood us – perhaps when we've expressed ourselves badly or rashly – or to have the kind of conversation that alerts us to the possibility that there may be gaps in our thinking.

A proper debate is good because it enables us to test our views while discovering where our thinking may not yet be fully formed. We can also, if we're open to it, better appreciate how someone with a different opinion has come to that position. A debate is very different from an argument, which usually seeks to bolster one's own standpoint while simultaneously demolishing the other's – there's far less that's constructive about an argument. Debate, on the other hand, is more nuanced. It retains an openness to listening and considering what the other has to say. We might even be willing to adjust our ideas – or the language we use to present them – as a result.

It's worth noting that much of what passes for debate on television is nothing of the kind. The programmes in question are now largely an arena for arguments: participants are often selected for the likelihood of their antagonizing one another and proceedings are cloaked with the trappings of a debate to lend credibility. When one participant rips into another with a good verbal kicking, the clip will go viral over social media the following day. The ancient gladiatorial arena is now online. The weapon of choice: opinions.

In the West we're fortunate to have a right to our opinion *and* to express it. I'm very glad such freedoms – mostly – exist. But some people today seem to feel that if you challenge their opinion you're somehow diminishing them as people. This is a real indicator of the limitations opinions have as a social currency, as a way of binding or dividing people. It's another example of how dualistic thinking disrupts our capacity to relate. We are not our opinions, and my affirmation of you as a person shouldn't hinge on whether or not you agree with me about Britain's place in the EU, the latest pop craze being all marketing and no talent or Adam's and Eve's existence being nothing more than an ancient mythical literary device – and so on.

It's sown into Christian spirituality that we accommodate the good *and* bad in others, as well as ourselves. By extension, good people can have a different outlook from you and still be good people. And a good person can say they think you're wrong, and that doesn't make them a bad person – or carry an implication that you are. Wouldn't it be great if the Church could be a better model of that kind of non-dualistic relating, or our media more inclined to present nuanced reporting? Contemporary society needs it. However, as Thomas Moore noted, society 'values opinion over reflection. It always wants to know who is right, and not who has the most interesting and suggestive ideas.'[1] Is it any wonder, when we're so bombarded with opinions, that we feel compelled to wade in and launch our own volley of views?

Opinions are a judgement, susceptible to the same shortcomings we explored earlier in Part 1 of the book. They present a perspective, informed only by whatever experiences or learning we've been exposed to. We must ask ourselves how much of the whole vista we have before us. Is it an expert view or only a tiny perspective? Do we consider ourselves well informed even when we've only read something in the newspaper or a blog, or had a chat with a couple of mates down the pub?

To love others means learning to see from their perspective before deciding what we think of their opinion. And, sometimes, silence is the better way, particularly when it aids a more reflective or contemplative approach to life. There's much ancient wisdom about this.

A Chinese scholar once observed that 'there is no seeking after truth; it is enough to stop holding opinions.'[2] While, in the sayings of the Desert Fathers, 'It was said about Abba Agathon that for three years he carried a pebble around in his mouth until he learned to be silent.'[3]

Francis de Sales reminds us of the consequences when we bandy around opinions of other people too freely:

Many take the liberty of judging others rashly, delighting in the sound of their own voice, opinions and wit. If unhappily, they err in their judgement, it then becomes very difficult to correct people's perspective because of the force and confidence with which opinions have been expressed.[4]

That quotation should be taped to the laptop of every columnist writing a newspaper opinion piece – and perhaps also stapled to my forehead.

It's sometimes discerning to keep the powder of our opinions dry until it's really necessary to offer a considered viewpoint, not sling them at anyone who'll listen as a way of validating ourselves.

My father was often a helpful presence in church meetings. Although a man of solid convictions, he rarely pushed his opinion to the forefront. He would sit and listen while others did that and then, towards the end of the discussion, offer a measured and restrained comment, often cutting through the polarity of opposing opinions. I might not often be like that myself, but I certainly aspire to be. Perhaps a pebble in the mouth . . . ?

But how and when do Christians decide when it's right to speak out? Surely I'm not building a case that suggests we simply try to build better relationships with people without, at times, drawing attention to what we see around us that seems wrong? Well, yes and no. There's a big difference between, say, blowing the whistle on where society, government or business are failing the common good, and moralizing at individuals to tell them to be more like us.

The Church's finger-wagging approach about personal morality has failed. Get the hint people. Nobody's listening, and shouting louder isn't going to make us any more heard. We've lost some of our moral authority, not least because our own house is so disordered – it's not just the scale of sexual abuse that's come to light, or how we've dragged our feet to affirm women's ministry, but that the Church has so often and for too long tried to manipulate and control people for its own ends. We have too often exercised the kind of spirit-crushing religious authority Jesus stood up to.

Giving in to the very human urge to set others straight was never what Christians were called to. Jesus said, 'Just as I have loved you, you also should love one another. *By this everyone will know that you are my disciples, if you have love for one another*' (John 13.34–35; emphasis added). Our witness comes from the example we set, the lives we live and the practical love we demonstrate – which of course is very much the hard and narrow road, and explains why an institution full of humans in all their brokenness and screwed-upness took the wide and easy road of judgement and finger-pointing.

When Jesus commissioned his followers to go out into the world and make disciples, he didn't mention anything about taking a soapbox along with them. The apostle Paul did, of course, go out into public squares – in a culture where that was the predominant form of mass media – and tell people how Jesus had transformed him. Much of his mission work was building up the first churches, helping them live out the countercultural and radical boundary-breaking, all-things-in-common, life of the kingdom of God.

Paul had a great personal testimony to tell, and let go of all the comforts of life to live out the gospel. As mendicant friars were to do centuries later, Paul was a sofa surfer depending on the hospitality of others to keep him housed and fed. There are those marvellous passages in 2 Corinthians where he lists all the hardships he faced for the sake of the gospel. One thing you could say about Paul: he put his money where his mouth was.

## Loving by example

If we really want to make people sit up and take note about the life-changing power of Christ's love, it won't be by scolding them. It will come from forming communities radically different from the neighbourhoods in which they exist; places of loving welcome and acceptance; a willingness to let go of our wealth and our comforts and share them with others; a habit of rolling up our sleeves and getting alongside the people whom nobody else wants to touch; celebrating what God has done in our lives rather than telling others what's wrong with theirs.

Whatever pronouncements Christians want to make will only have integrity when they're living, breathing examples of life the Jesus way. Which isn't to suggest we have to be perfect. We can't be – but surely we can do a bit better?

Of course, the lives of some Christians are excellent examples. When my church goes out carol singing at Christmas, it's J's job to give out leaflets about our Christmas services. By her own admission she has a singing voice like a bath draining, so the ministry of leafleting is very much geared to her talents. But – and I promise this is no exaggeration – by the end of the first carol she'll be nowhere to be seen. She'll have found a homeless person and will either be ringing the Street Team to arrange a bed for the night or rummaging around in her bag looking for a banana to hand out (which is why I've learned it's always best to have a second person handing out leaflets).

Or take my parents, who are now old enough to need some extra support. The family do a massive amount yet can't always be there due to work and other commitments. But a couple from my parents' church call in regularly to sit with them, help out with little tasks or drive them to appointments – quietly, faithfully and with real loving dedication.

Actually I know quite a few Christians like that. They're often found in churches but we haven't yet reached a critical mass where most of our congregations are characterized by such behaviour. Perhaps we haven't nurtured this kind of practical witness enough because we've been so busy telling people off or squabbling over theology. The urge to deliver judgements doesn't sit well with the kind of witness that modestly gets on and leads by example. Jim Wallis writes:

> When [a church] doesn't just righteously proclaim itself to be 'pro-life' but quietly takes in hundreds of low-income pregnant women every year to help them carry their children to term and settle into a better life, people feel helped and not just judged.[5]

Christians are called to action rather than judgement. Pope Francis has spoken out about the Roman Catholic Church being too obsessed

with issues of sexuality, abortion and contraception and not focusing enough on making the Church a 'home for all'.[6]

It may or may not have been Mahatma Gandhi who said,
'Become the change you want to see in the world', but I do
rather wish Jesus had said it – we might be more willing to paint
it on the walls of our churches. I'm not, however, arguing that
the Church has no role in speaking out on what's wrong with the
world. Although I am bothered about our obsession with putting
others right, I do very firmly believe that prophetic witness is part
of the Church's mission.

## Prophetic witness

The Church has too often tried to avoid being political and focused
instead on the personal. Doing so runs the risk of allowing us to
pull down the shutters on issues of social justice while busily
preaching against all the things in society we believe immoral.
That's not prophetic witness – living in tune with the kingdom
of God demands action and lifestyle changes too.

Hearteningly, the Church has sometimes proved extremely good
at this prophetic stuff. The Jubilee 2000 campaign marshalled
thousands of Christians to lobby for the cancellation of debt in
the Global South; more recently there have been excellent Church-
led campaigns on modern slavery and sexual trafficking. These
campaigns are often costly, requiring people to give up time, energy
and resources to get organized, write, lobby, demonstrate. Such
activities make the Church more attractive to young people –
woefully absent in many congregations – who are otherwise
naturally averse to older folk who talk the talk but don't back it
up with action.

Prophetic witness tackles systems that are unjust and oppress
the most vulnerable, especially the poor, who, as we've seen, Jesus
calls us to take particular care of. Rather than focusing on the
personal it tackles the mechanisms and arrangements by which
big business, government, international relations, economics, law
and so on operate – in the course of which it's often the least powerful who are chewed up or neglected. These are the principalities

and powers of whom Paul writes in Ephesians: 'For our struggle is not against enemies of blood and flesh, but against the rulers, against the authorities, against the cosmic powers of this present darkness, against the spiritual forces of evil in the heavenly places' (Ephesians 6.12). As Walter Wink has written extensively and cogently in his 'Powers' trilogy, such principalities and powers 'are the inner and outer aspects of any given manifestation of power'. He goes on:

> As the inner aspect they are the spirituality of institutions, the 'within' of corporate structures and systems, the inner essence of outer organizations of power. As the outer aspect they are political systems, appointed officials, the 'chair' of an organization, laws – in short, all the tangible manifestations which power takes. Every Power tends to have a visible pole, an outer form – be it a church, a nation, or an economy – and an invisible pole, an inner spirit or driving force that animates, legitimates, and regulates its physical manifestation in the world . . . When a particular Power becomes idolatrous, placing itself above God's purposes for the good of the whole, then that Power becomes demonic. The church's task is to unmask this idolatry and recall the Powers to their created purposes in the world.[7]

Prophetic witness identifies these systemic demons and exposes them for what they are. This is where the Church's finger-pointing can legitimately be directed, not unlike the Old Testament prophets who would regularly rock up to the palace to offer a State of the Nation address, pointing out the injustices and corruption of their day. For us today there's plenty in our world that goes wrong because of the way governments, institutions and corporations exercise power, manipulate the disadvantaged, lure us to overconsume or leverage wealth for their own benefit. But we should remember that there are a lot of good people working within these systems.

Owen Jones is the author of *The Establishment: And How They Get Away With It*, in which he argues that the powers that be who control Britain do so in ways that serve their own interests rather than the common good. In the course of researching the book he interviewed a number of establishment figures and had this to say about them:

> These are not bad people. The answer is not to get rid of them and replace them with good people. It is the system that is wrong and we must organize ourselves to campaign for a change in the systems that perpetuate injustice.[8]

We could learn a lot from that. And this is how Jesus operated, calling out evil in the institutions and structures around him that oppressed the people. This is also what many of his healing miracles symbolize. Brian McLaren writes:

> Thousands come to Jesus with various afflictions and internal oppressions, and Jesus draws into the light whatever oppressive, destructive, disease-causing, imbalancing, paralyzing, or convulsing forces hide within them so they can be freed and restored to balance and health ... [T]he demonic gives us a language to personify and identify these covert forces that enter groups of us, using us, becoming a guiding part of us, possessing and influencing and even controlling us.[9]

Jesus' prophetic witness can be seen when he throws the money changers out of the temple or when he points out the hypocrisy of religious leadership that works hard to appear spotless on the outside but is slowly rotting from within. He challenges those controlled by their wealth and upsets the social norms of the day by drawing into fellowship those society shuns. Ultimately he exposes the evil of the Roman Empire and its puppet king, Herod, by handing himself over to them so they can be seen for what they are.

This is our mission, and if we've been weak on it perhaps it's because our energy has been diverted in the wrong direction, taking up causes that are easy to talk about – the lives of others – rather than the costly, risky and personally demanding road of prophetic witness. When we do get it right, we're brilliant. We set aside our denominational differences and theological squabbles and pull together to take on demonic forces that tread on the poorest and most vulnerable. Collectively we discern where the common good isn't being served and expose it. We're not required to judge it, simply show it up for what it is.

I remember the much-missed Mike Yaconelli speaking at Greenbelt about the satirical magazine *The Wittenberg Door*, which he edited. The focus of its humour was the Church, and Mike talked about the way he felt satire could be constructive. He believed the most powerful form of satire was not to ridicule people or even comment on them but simply to reprint what they'd said or done and let it speak for itself. That's a kind of prophetic witness – it doesn't judge, it just holds up to the light something that's fatuous, hypocritical, unjust or deceitful. (Some of the satire in *Private Eye* magazine works like this: here's a newspaper column by a journalist declaiming the sexualization of children; and here, right next to it, a piece about what an attractive young women a certain 17-year-old starlet's turning into – complete with photos of her in a cropped top or swimsuit. You don't even need to write a headline – just turn a spotlight on the hypocrisy.)

Not many of us are called to satire, so the Church exercises much of its prophetic witness through the organizations we set up. Bodies like Christian Aid, the Children's Society, the Food Bank network or Church Urban Fund conduct research and bring to light how government policy, funding cuts, international trade agreements, business practices – and much more – impact on the lives of some of the most vulnerable people. It's vital work that enables the Church to speak truth to power, simply through presenting the facts or the consequences of current policies and practices. Of course, as well as campaigning on such issues they also provide practical help or support to those in need. They have moral authority because they don't just talk about what's wrong, they do something about it too. Prophetic witness like this has real integrity.

Back in our pews we mustn't simply delegate prophetic witness to these specialists. It's great that we help fund their people to do research, campaign or take practical action – that helps us be properly informed and grounded. But to fulfil our calling we must also join in.

By rechannelling our energies and focusing on the common good, Christians can be a force for change. Individually we can roll up our sleeves to feed the hungry, welcome the stranger and visit the imprisoned. Collectively we can get in tune with our brothers and sisters across church traditions to find a combined prophetic voice – and use it.

For this to be really effective requires three aspects of Christian life to work together in harmony:

- speaking truth to power;
- loving action;
- generous spirituality.

Our prophetic voice will only have integrity in exposing that which stands in the way of the common good when we're living out the gospel in our own lives, demonstrating 'love thy neighbour' in our day-to-day practical action. But our voice and action must be animated by a third dimension, a generous spirituality driven by the indwelling of God's Spirit. Not a dualistic, competitive, judgemental head-faith but a centring on God's grace and love for all of creation.

## Contemplative prayer

For me, one approach to cultivating such a way of being has emerged as offering the key to breaking the cycle of judgmental thinking, and that is the practice of contemplative prayer.

As I'm still a novice at this, I'll let Richard Rohr describe the difference it makes:

How you see anything is how you see everything. How you do this moment is how you do every moment. If, right now, you are listening to me and you are trying to prove how I am wrong, why I am wrong, and you are marshalling your arguments to disprove whatever it is I am saying ... I just want to warn you of this. That if you are doing this right now with me, I would be willing to bet that you do that with your wife, your husband, your children, with your neighbourhood, with your church, with your politics. That is the way you do the moment. You tear it apart. You critique it. That is your way of defending yourself from truth, from anything that might lead you outside your comfort zone. [But] the contemplative wants the truth so badly, wants God so badly, wants the good and the true and the beautiful so badly that they dare to leave the field of the moment open. They refuse to label it . . . or categorize it.[10]

Rohr describes how contemplative prayer helps to break the pattern of the judgemental mind. The constant chattering inside one's head gives a running commentary on whatever and whoever we encounter. It is the servant of judgement. At its worse this can turn inwards, leading to anxiety or depression.

We could all, I'm sure, do with some space and silence to recuperate from the barrage of words that fill our days. Even our church services are too full of words, with precious little silence (unless you're a Quaker). And when words are filling our heads, even when there's nobody else in the room, then we become bound up by a narrative that's 'defensive, oppositional, paranoid and self-referential'.[11]

Contemplative prayer moves us into a space that's open to the presence of God and present to the moment. It's a practised stillness that's attentive and non-judgemental. Interestingly, under the guise of 'mindfulness', the National Health Service is now offering classes in a secular variation of this, as treatment for stress, depression and anxiety. In contemplation, however, we bring this practice into the realm of the divine. Our aim is 'to be deeply available to God . . . [simply] to attend, to give yourself completely into that deeper, mysterious presence'.[12]

Sometimes also called Christian meditation or centring prayer, contemplation offers a chance to suspend the chattering mind, and over time the potential to retrain the judgemental and dualistic mind.

Thomas Keating has done much to teach a method of centring prayer – there are online resources to help you learn it.[13] And Stephen Cottrell's book *Do Nothing to Change Your Life* makes an excellent introductory case for spending time in silence each day.[14]

When we centre ourselves on God's absolute loving acceptance for us, bit by bit we can retrain the judgemental mind to offer that same loving acceptance to others – and ourselves. No need to compete, compare, judge better or worse – simply allow ourselves to be open to our 'fellow peripherals', to take the moment as it comes, and see what it has to offer us.

It may take years of practice to let go of the judgemental mind. But when we stop to remind ourselves how diminished we are by our judgementalism, what better motivation could there be?

# Notes

## 1 The urge to judge

1 <www.theguardian.com/uk-news/2014/aug/15/cliff-richard-leak-bbc-police-deny>.
2 Desmond Tutu and Mpho Tutu, *Made for Goodness: And Why This Makes All the Difference*, London: Rider, 2010, p. 6.
3 Eugene H. Peterson, *The Message Remix: The Bible in Contemporary Language*, Colorado Springs, CO: NavPress, 2003.
4 *Desert Wisdom: Sayings from the Desert Fathers*, trans. Yushi Nomura, Maryknoll, NY: Orbis, 2001, p. 7.
5 Francis de Sales, *Introduction to the Devout Life*, III, 28–29, from *Celebrating the Seasons: Daily Spiritual Readings for the Christian Year*, compiled Robert Atwell, Norwich: Canterbury Press, 1999.
6 Richard Foster, *Celebration of Discipline: The Path to Spiritual Growth*, London: Hodder & Stoughton, 2008, p. 10.

## 2 Tribalism

1 Quoted in Desmond Tutu and Mpho Tutu, *Made for Goodness: And Why This Makes All the Difference*, London: Rider, 2010, p. 14.
2 Timothy Radcliffe, *Why Go to Church? The Drama of the Eucharist*, London: Continuum, 2008, p. 60.
3 Richard Rohr, *The Art of Letting Go* (audio download), Louisville, CO: Sounds True, 2010, my transcription.
4 Rohr, *Art of Letting Go*.
5 Rohr, *Art of Letting Go*.
6 Richard Cleaver, *Know My Name: A Gay Liberation Theology*, Louisville, KY: Westminster John Knox Press, 1995, p. 85.
7 Cleaver, *Know My Name*, p. 87.
8 Sara Miles, *Take This Bread: A Radical Conversion*, New York: Ballantine Books, 2007, pp. 76–7.

## 3 Fear

1 <www.facebook.com/TheDailyMailListOfThingsThatGiveYouCancer/info>, retrieved 9 September 2014.

2 Scott Bader-Saye, *Following Jesus in a Culture of Fear*, Grand Rapids, MI: Brazos Press, 2007, p. 21.
3 Quoted in Bader-Saye, *Following Jesus*, p. 28.
4 Bader-Saye, *Following Jesus*, p. 12.
5 James Alison, *Faith Beyond Resentment: Fragments Catholic and Gay*, London: Darton, Longman & Todd, 2001, p. 100.
6 <www.hymntime.com/tch/htm/w/e/h/wehavean.htm>.
7 Attributed to the writer Katherine Anne Porter (1890–1980).

# 4 Blame and scapegoating

1 Jim Wallis, *On God's Side: What Religion Forgets and Politics Hasn't Learned about Serving the Common Good*, Grand Rapids, MI: Brazos, 2013, pp. 159–60.
2 *Benedictine Daily Prayer: A Short Breviary*, Dublin: Columba Press, 2005, p. 1115.
3 Thomas Merton, *New Seeds of Contemplation*, New York: New Directions, 2007, p. 112.
4 Quoted in Thomas Moore, *Dark Nights of the Soul: A Guide to Finding Your Way through Life's Ordeals*, New York: Gotham Books, 2004, p. 115.
5 Richard Rohr, *Yes, And . . . Daily Meditations*, Cincinnati, OH: Franciscan Media, 2013, p. 237.
6 Moore, *Dark Nights of the Soul*, p. 67.

# 5 Pride and ignorance

1 C. S. Lewis, *Mere Christianity*, London: Collins, 2012 (first published 1952), pp. 124–5.
2 St Augustine, from his treatise 'On the Trinity', VIII, viii (12), from *Celebrating the Seasons: Daily Spiritual Readings for the Christian Year*, compiled Robert Atwell, Norwich: Canterbury Press, 1999.
3 Francis de Sales, *Introduction to the Devout Life*, III, 28–29, from *Celebrating the Seasons*.
4 de Sales, *Introduction to the Devout Life*, III, 28–29.
5 Cynthia Bourgeault, *The Wisdom Jesus: Transforming Heart and Mind – A New Perspective on Christ and His Message*, Boston, MA: Shambhala, 2008, pp. 36–7.
6 Fraser Dyer, *Why Do I Do This Every Day? Finding Meaning in Your Work*, Oxford: Lion, 2005, p. 139.
7 Thomas Merton, *New Seeds of Contemplation*, New York: New Directions, 2007, p. 116.

# 6 Shame and self-judgement

1 Alan Downs, *The Velvet Rage: Overcoming the Pain of Growing Up Gay in a Straight Man's World*, 2nd edn, Boston, MA: De Capo Press, 2012, pp. 185–6.

2 From the title of John Bradshaw's book, *Healing the Shame that Binds You*, Deerfield Beach, FL: Health Communications, 1988.

3 Daniel Migliore, *Faith Seeking Understanding: An Introduction to Christian Theology*, 2nd edn, Grand Rapids, MI: Eerdmans, 2004.

4 Francis Spufford, *Unapologetic: Why Despite Everything Christianity Can Still Make Surprising Emotional Sense*, London: Faber & Faber, 2012, p. 63.

5 Robert Farrar Capon, *Kingdom, Grace, Judgment: Paradox, Outrage, and Vindication in the Parables of Jesus*, Grand Rapids, MI: Eerdmans, 2002, pp. 349–50.

6 Thomas Moore, *Dark Nights of the Soul: A Guide to Finding Your Way through Life's Ordeals*, New York: Gotham Books, 2004, p. 101.

7 American senator Daniel Patrick Moynihan, quoted in Alan Johnson, 'I've never sought the Labour leadership – and I never will', *The Guardian*, 10 November 2014, <www.theguardian.com/commentisfree/2014/nov/10/alan-johnson-labour-leadership-ed-miliband-loyalty>.

8 Desmond Tutu and Mpho Tutu, *Made for Goodness: And Why This Makes All the Difference*, London: Rider, 2010, p. 176.

9 Timothy Radcliffe, *Why Go to Church? The Drama of the Eucharist*, London: Continuum, 2008, p. 41.

# 7 How did Christians become so judgemental?

1 David Sedaris, 'If I ruled the world', *Prospect*, 22 February 2012, <www.prospectmagazine.co.uk/regulars/if-i-ruled-the-world-david-sedaris>.

2 Timothy Radcliffe, *What Is the Point of Being a Christian?*, London: Burns & Oates, 2005, p. 4.

3 Tom Wright, *Matthew for Everyone, Part 1: Chapters 1–15*, London: SPCK, 2002, p. 67.

4 Wright, *Matthew for Everyone, Part 1*, p. 70.

5 Reflection by Barbara Mosse in *Reflections for Daily Prayer: Advent 2013 to Eve of Advent 2014*, London: Church House Publishing, 2013.

6 James Alison, *On Being Liked*, London: Darton, Longman & Todd, 2003, p. 73.

7 Jim Wallis, *On God's Side: What Religion Forgets and Politics Hasn't Learned about Serving the Common Good*, Grand Rapids, MI: Brazos, 2013, p. 65.

## 8 The judge judged

1 Karl Barth, *Church Dogmatics*, vol. IV.1, §59.2, London: T. & T. Clark, 2010, pp. 232, 220.
2 Barth, *Church Dogmatics*, vol. IV.1, §59.2, p. 232.
3 Barth, *Church Dogmatics*, vol. IV.1, §59.2, p. 17.
4 Barth, *Church Dogmatics*, vol. IV.1, §59.2, p. 221.

## 9 Breaking down barriers

1 Desmond Tutu, *God Has a Dream: A Vision of Hope for Our Time*, London: Rider, 2004, p. 32.
2 Reflection by Paul Kennedy, *Reflections for Daily Prayer: Advent 2013 to Eve of Advent 2014*, London: Church House Publishing, 2013.
3 Eugene H. Peterson, *The Message Remix: The Bible in Contemporary Language*, Colorado Springs, CO: NavPress, 2003.
4 Catherine Pepinster, 'Justice, tempered by mercy', *The Guardian*, 21 August 2010, <www.theguardian.com/commentisfree/belief/2010/aug/21/compassion-religion>.

## 10 The offer of loving acceptance

1 Brian D. McLaren, *The Secret Message of Jesus: Uncovering the Truth That Could Change Everything*, Nashville, TN: Nelson, 2006, p. 94.

## 11 Seeing ourselves, and others, for who we really are

1 Cynthia Bourgeault, *The Wisdom Jesus: Transforming Heart and Mind – A New Perspective on Christ and His Message*, Boston, MA: Shambhala, 2008, p. 11.
2 Bourgeault, *The Wisdom Jesus*, p. 11.
3 Tom Wright, *John for Everyone, Part 1: Chapters 1–10*, 2nd edn, London: SPCK, 2004, p. 113.
4 Francis Spufford, *Unapologetic: Why Despite Everything Christianity Can Still Make Surprising Emotional Sense*, London: Faber & Faber, 2012, p. 118, emphasis in original.
5 Thomas Moore, *Dark Nights of the Soul: A Guide to Finding your Way through Life's Ordeals*, New York: Gotham Books, 2004, p. 71.

## 12 Tearing the doors off their hinges

1 Cynthia Bourgeault, *The Wisdom Jesus: Transforming Heart and Mind – A New Perspective on Christ and His Message*, Boston, MA: Shambhala, 2008, p. 49.

2 Francis Spufford, *Unapologetic: Why Despite Everything Christianity Can Still Make Surprising Emotional Sense*, London: Faber & Faber, 2012, pp. 177–8.
3 Spufford, *Unapologetic*, pp. 178–9.
4 Robert Farrar Capon, *Kingdom, Grace, Judgment: Paradox, Outrage, and Vindication in the Parables of Jesus*, Grand Rapids, MI: Eerdmans, 2002, p. 460.
5 Capon, *Kingdom, Grace, Judgment*, p. 65.
6 Anthony de Mello, *Seek God Everywhere: Reflections on the Spiritual Exercises of St. Ignatius*, New York: Doubleday, 2010, p. 25.
7 Tom Wright, *Luke for Everyone*, 2nd edn, London: SPCK, 2004, p. 170.
8 Spufford, *Unapologetic*, p. 63.

## 13 Getting at the truth

1 Collect for St Barnabas, *Common Worship: Festivals*, London: Church House Publishing, 2008, p. 74.
2 'Martin Scorsese pays tribute to Philip French', *The Guardian*, 25 August 2013, <www.theguardian.com/film/2013/aug/25/martin-scorsese-tribute-philip-french>.
3 Quoted in 'Mark Kermode to become the Observer's chief film critic', *The Guardian*, 17 August 2013, <www.theguardian.com/media/2013/aug/17/mark-kermode-film-critic-observer>.
4 Reflection by Malcolm Guite, *Reflections for Daily Prayer: Advent 2011 to Eve of Advent 2012*, London: Church House Publishing, 2011.
5 N. T. Wright and Marcus Borg, *The Meaning of Jesus*, London: SPCK, 1999.

## 14 Discernment

1 Reflection by Malcolm Guite, *Reflections for Daily Prayer: Advent 2011 to Eve of Advent 2012*, London: Church House Publishing, 2011.
2 Desmond Tutu and Mpho Tutu, *Made for Goodness: And Why This Makes All the Difference*, London: Rider, 2010, p. 7.
3 David Lonsdale, *Eyes to See, Ears to Hear: An Introduction to Ignatian Spirituality*, London: Darton, Longman & Todd, 1990, p. 89.
4 <http://en.wikipedia.org/wiki/Prayer_of_Saint_Francis>.
5 Samuel Wells, personal communication in respect of Wells, *God's Companions: Reimagining Christian Ethics*, Oxford: Blackwell, 2006.
6 Rudyard Kipling, 'I Keep Six Honest Serving-Men', in *Animal Stories*, Kelly Bray, Cornwall: House of Stratus, 2001, p. 134.
7 James Martin, *The Jesuit Guide to (Almost) Everything: A Spirituality for Real Life*, New York: HarperCollins, 2010, pp. 234–5, emphasis/italics in original.

8 Francis de Sales, *Introduction to the Devout Life*, III, 28–29, from *Celebrating the Seasons: Daily Spiritual Readings for the Christian Year*, compiled Robert Atwell, Norwich: Canterbury Press, 1999.

9 Dietrich Bonhoeffer, *Life Together*, trans. John W. Doberstein, New York: Harper & Row, 1954, p. 30.

10 Martin, *Jesuit Guide to (Almost) Everything*, p. 88.

11 Lucy Lind Hogan, 'Commentary on 1 Thessalonians 5:16–24', <www.workingpreacher.org/preaching.aspx?commentary_id=2280>.

## 15 Prophetic witness

1 Thomas Moore, *Dark Nights of the Soul: A Guide to Finding Your Way through Life's Ordeals*, New York: Gotham Books, 2004, p. 32.

2 Source unknown.

3 *Desert Wisdom: Sayings from the Desert Fathers*, trans. Yushi Nomura, Maryknoll, NY: Orbis, 2001, p. 5.

4 Francis de Sales, *Introduction to the Devout Life*, III, 28–29, from *Celebrating the Seasons: Daily Spiritual Readings for the Christian Year*, compiled Robert Atwell, Norwich: Canterbury Press, 1999.

5 Jim Wallis, *On God's Side: What Religion Forgets and Politics Hasn't Learned about Serving the Common Good*, Grand Rapids, MI: Brazos, 2013, p. 23.

6 <www.huffingtonpost.com/2013/09/19/pope-francis-gay_n_3954776.html>, retrieved 20 January 2015.

7 Walter Wink, *Naming The Powers: The Language of Power in the New Testament*, Philadelphia, PA: Fortress Press, 1984, p. 5.

8 Owen Jones, in a talk at the Bishopsgate Institute, 6 November 2014, my transcription; podcast at <www.bishopsgate.org.uk/audios.aspx?vid=9501>.

9 Brian D. McLaren, *The Secret Message of Jesus: Uncovering the Truth that Could Change Everything*, Nashville, TN: Nelson, 2006, pp. 63–4.

10 Richard Rohr, *The Art of Letting Go* (audio download), Louisville, CO: Sounds True, 2010, my transcription.

11 Rohr, *Art of Letting Go*.

12 Cynthia Bourgeault, *The Wisdom Jesus: Transforming Heart and Mind – A New Perspective on Christ and His Message*, Boston, MA: Shambhala, 2008, p. 143.

13 See, for example, the downloadable PDF document 'Method of Centering Prayer' at <www.contemplativeoutreach.org/category/category/centering-prayer>.

14 Stephen Cottrell, *Do Nothing to Change Your Life: Discovering What Happens When You Stop*, London: Church House Publishing, 2007.